MATTHEW

WESLEY BIBLE STUDIES

D1407616

wphonline.com

CONTENTS

INTRODUCTION
Lessons from the Master

Three-and-a-half years is not a long time. It is barely enough time to embark on a world-changing venture, let alone complete one. Yet in just that short length of time, Jesus Christ defined a way of life through His words and actions that radically altered the course of human history.

There are many ways to approach the study of Christ. Some approaches would focus on His self-understanding, rightly emphasizing His identity as the Son of God, the second person of the Trinity. Others would examine the deeds of Jesus, emphasizing the divine power displayed through His miracles and justifiably celebrating His resurrection from the dead. Either approach would yield an accurate picture of Christ and lead students to truth.

Our approach will be slightly different, however. In this study, we will focus on the *words* of Jesus, examining some of His most powerful teachings as recorded by Matthew, the tax collector turned apostle. Here are some of the takeaways you will discover in these powerful lessons.

GOD'S BLESSING COMES IN UNLIKELY WAYS

Jesus' masterwork of theology, the passage of Scripture we know as the Sermon on the Mount, provides the context for four studies in this book. In the Beatitudes, those beautiful yet disturbing pronouncements of blessing, Jesus teaches us that God's best for us is not always what we would consider best for ourselves. The more we try to impress others, the less we impress God. The more we seek for ourselves, the less we are likely to gain. God's view of the world and our view are, well, different. Jesus teaches us that our best hope for a happy life, both now and later, is to trust God with childlike faith. That doesn't come naturally to most of us. These readings will challenge you to make your life more like Christ in everyday ways.

FOLLOWING JESUS CALLS FOR TOTAL COMMITMENT

The cost of discipleship is a favorite subject for Jesus. Realizing that many of the eager crowds who followed Him during the early days of His ministry were more interested in *show* than in *grow*, Jesus intentionally upped the ante for His followers. To be a disciple of Christ calls for an open mind, total commitment, and complete obedience.

While we say that our world is ever changing, the human penchant for easy solutions and nominal commitment seems constant. In this study, you will be challenged to examine the strength of your faith and the depth of your commitment to Jesus Christ.

AS CHANGED PEOPLE, WE CHANGE THE WORLD

The gospel is powerful and effective. It will have an effect upon your life, and you, in turn, will have a revolutionary effect upon the world. Over and over, Jesus made these points in His teaching. Yes, you really can enjoy God's blessing. Yes, it is possible to fully and freely forgive those who have wronged you. Better yet, this new society we have formed—this kingdom of heaven—will grow from just a few comrades in faith to become a great force in the world. When you forgive, when you love others, when you perform acts of kindness in the name of Jesus Christ, you are quite literally changing the world. You will be motivated to allow God's grace to work in your life and to offer that grace to others.

In this study, we have the pleasure of studying both the first arrival of Jesus, as a child in Bethlehem, and His second advent, as the Judge of all the earth. Let these words from Christ move you the way they moved His first hearers—to experience God's blessing in surprising ways.

1

THE BIRTH OF JESUS

Matthew 1:18–25

The birth of Jesus brings the hope of salvation from sin.

Probably no event in the history of the world is more widely known or more eagerly celebrated than the birth of Jesus Christ. It is the centerpiece of the calendar in many parts of the world, dividing time into two great eras—Before Christ (B.C.) and *Anno Domini* (A.D., the year of our Lord). Children and adults alike look forward to the celebration of Christ's birth, when schools and businesses are closed and we take a holiday from the cares of life.

This study will enrich your celebration of this grand event by lifting your eyes beyond Christmases past to the ongoing work of Jesus in the world. As we remember the birth of our Lord, we'll gain new hope for the salvation of humankind.

COMMENTARY

Since Matthew was written primarily to a Jewish audience, it is appropriate for the story of Jesus' birth to stem from Joseph's perspective. Jesus' lineage is traced through His legal father, Joseph, although Matthew made it clear that Joseph was not Jesus' biological father.

Joseph Learned Mary Was Expecting a Baby (Matt. 1:18–19)

In first-century Jewish society, engagements were as serious affairs as marriage. Breaking them required a "divorce." Since **Mary was pledged to be married to Joseph** (v. 18), her pregnancy was taken as evidence of adultery. Joseph was torn between righteousness and love. He had been wronged and considered Mary untrust-worthy and unfit to marry, but he refused **to expose her to public disgrace** (v. 19) by making a formal complaint and a claim for damages before her parents and the whole village. All that was necessary for a **divorce** (v. 19) in those days was for the husband to write a simple letter, have it signed by two witnesses, and have it delivered to his wife. In making this decision, Joseph accepted a financial loss in addition to his feelings of shame and betrayal. By refusing to take Mary to court, he would have lost the "bride price" he paid her parents, as well as Mary's dowry, which he had the right to keep in the case of divorce due to adultery.

Joseph's initial decision to divorce Mary was not harsh or unjust from their perspective. In the ancient world, a man was obligated by custom and social pressure (and in some cases, by law) to divorce a wife who had committed adultery. If he did not, he would be despised as weak and not caring enough for honor. A wife (or fiancée) who was unfaithful brought on her husband (or betrothed) one of the greatest possible causes for personal hurt and public shame. Mosaic law provided stiff penalties for adultery, and though the death sentence would likely not be carried out in the first century, the crime was still treated very seriously.

Mary's pregnancy, however, was not through any human father. It was from **the Holy Spirit** (v. 18). This would be unlike any other human birth. It reminds us of the miraculous births of Isaac, Jacob and Esau, and Samuel, but even greater.

The Angel Told Joseph Who the Baby Was (Matt. 1:20–21)

Joseph's mind was changed by a vision in a dream, in which an angel addressed him. He was called **son of David** (v. 20) to stress his royal lineage, and that his "son" (who would actually be an adopted son as far as Joseph was concerned) would be eligible for the throne of Israel. **Do not be afraid** (v. 20) is a phrase of comfort, but not due to fear of angels; the fear Joseph would have to overcome was either of Mary's infidelity or the disgrace that would fall on him for marrying a woman the community now considered sinful. And for the second time Matthew emphasizes that the child within Mary had been created by **the Holy Spirit** (v. 20). Though Matthew's and Luke's gospels differ considerably on which details of Jesus' birth and infancy they narrate, they both agree on these things: Mary was a virgin; she was engaged to Joseph; the conception was a miracle caused by God's Spirit; an angel announced it to both Mary and Joseph; it is predicted that the child will be a boy, and He is named Jesus ahead of time by the angel; and there is a suggestion He will be Messiah.

The name **Jesus** (v. 21) is an old Hebrew name. Jesus is actually the Greek form of the name in the New Testament (*Iēsous*), but the Hebrew version of this name known to Jesus' parents was Joshua (*Yeshua'*), which means "Yahweh is salvation." Although many others had this name before and during the first century, it is still especially symbolic because (a) the name is predetermined by God via His messenger and (b) the mysterious, miraculous birth requires an explanation. The name predicts the Son's character and His mission: He is to be called "Yahweh is salvation," **because he will save his people from their sins** (v. 21). The **because** shows already before His birth this child was destined to be a manifestation of the God of Israel. The Jews expected the Messiah to save them in a political sense: liberation from Roman rule, national independence leading to Israel becoming a world power. He was also thought of as one who would lead the nation to religious purity and righteousness. But this is a different concept. That this Messiah's salvation will be to deliver God's people **from their sins** reminds us of the mission of the Suffering Servant of Isaiah 52:13—53:12, who "bore the sin of many, and made intercession for the transgressors" (53:12).

WORDS FROM WESLEY

Matthew 1:21

Let all adore the immortal King,
Maker of heaven and earth!
Angels and men, rejoice and sing
For your Creator's birth.
A Son is born, a Child is given,
That mortals born again
May in the new-created heaven
With God in glory reign.
Salvation from our sins we found,
Through Jesus' grace forgiven;
And Jesus' grace doth more abound,
And makes us meet for heaven:
The hallowing virtue of His name
Our spotless souls shall prove,
And to the utmost saved, proclaim
Our Lord's almighty love.
Jesus *from*, not *in*, our sins
Doth still His people save:
Him our Advocate and Prince,
Our Priest and King we have;
Strength in Him with righteousness,
With pardon purity, we gain,
Priests His praying Spirit possess,
And kings for ever reign. (PW, vol. 10, 140)

Matthew was keen to point out that Jesus' birth, as many other facets of His ministry, happened in fulfillment of prophecy (Matt. 1:22–23). Fulfillment is an idea Matthew was very interested in. The verb *fulfill* occurs fifteen times in this gospel (1:22; 2:15, 17, 23; 3:15; 4:14; 5:17; 8:17; 12:17; 13:14, 35; 21:4; 26:54, 56; 27:9), eleven of them introducing a quotation from the Old Testament. In addition, the Old Testament is cited directly another seven times (2:5; 4:4, 7, 10; 11:10; 21:13; 26:31), not counting general allusions to the Law or the Prophets, all of which shows Matthew's (and Jesus') keen interest in the

Scriptures we now call the Old Testament. Matthew wanted to emphasize that God foresaw and announced ahead of time the nature of Jesus' coming as the Messiah. Matthew also emphasized the link between old and new covenants: Faith in Jesus is not really a "new religion," even though it is a new working of God. Jesus' coming brought to completion God's intentions for Israel and all humanity as had already been announced through the prophets. In Jesus we see God's final saving intervention in human history to heal the wound of sin, and at the same time He displays for us in Jesus' life the ideal righteousness to which the law pointed. In these senses, Jesus has come "to fulfill" the law (Matt. 5:17).

The Baby Fulfilled the Prophecy (Matt. 1:22–23)

The prophet (v. 22) Matthew cites is Isaiah. For over a hundred years there has been debate about Matthew's use of Isaiah here. Isaiah 7 does not seem to have been understood as a messianic prophecy by Jews prior to Christianity. And a close reading of this text leads many scholars to assert that Isaiah's prediction had to do with the immediate future of eighth-century B.C. Judah: "But before the boy knows enough to reject the wrong and choose the right, the land of the two kings you dread will be laid waste" (Isa. 7:16). In other words, Ahaz was told that before this predicted "son" was old enough to have moral sense; the nations of Israel and Syria (who were threatening Judah) would be devastated. Some believed the prophecy referred to the birth of Hezekiah; others, to the birth of a son of Isaiah. Further, it is sometimes asserted that the original Hebrew term Isaiah used at 7:14 was not a technical term for virgin, but merely meant a young woman. Hence, it is said, Matthew is wrong on two counts: The text is not about a virgin, and it is not a prediction of a messiah in the distant future.

In response to these problems, a few insights can be offered. First, the Hebrew word Isaiah 7:14 used is *'almah*. Although not a technical term for virgin, it functions like the old English term *maiden*. In other words, unless the speaker gives some specific clue otherwise, the term normally refers to a young unmarried woman, which in that culture carried with it the presumption of virginity. *'Almah* never refers to a married woman in the Hebrew Old Testament. Some five hundred years later, when the Hebrew Old Testament was translated into Greek (the Septuagint), it was Jewish—not Christian—translators who chose the Greek term for *virgin* (*parthenos*) to translate this term. It is very possible that the Septuagint translators already believed this text would have a second, greater fulfillment when the Messiah came, the same way other texts that originally referred to a king (see Pss. 2; 110) were widely believed in Jesus' day to describe the coming Messiah.

Still, why would Matthew seize on this particular text? The only reasonable answer is that Matthew began with the historical fact that Mary was a virgin when she conceived Jesus by a miracle of God. Jews did not expect the Messiah to come from a virgin or to be divine. There is no reason Jesus' first followers (who were Jews) should have thought it necessary to claim these things about Him unless they were true. It was the unique and surprising way God had worked in bringing His Son to us that caused Jesus' disciples to search their Scriptures afresh for the "clues" to the Messiah that they had previously overlooked. Matthew pointed us to Isaiah because he was now reading his Bible through the lens of Christ's life.

Some skeptics like to claim that this birth story is no different from pagan myths from Greece and Rome that speak of gods mating with human women and producing demigods or heroes such as Hercules or Dionysus; or they compare it to the story of how Alexander the Great was born. But such myths always have one thing in common: The event occurs because of the carnal lust of a god who assumes some physical shape and has intercourse with a woman—usually against her will. Yet there is no hint whatsoever of any physical passion between God and Mary. The language carefully avoids any such innuendo. Instead, the style of the story is more like that of the miraculous conceptions of Isaac and Samuel than anything else.

WORDS FROM WESLEY
Matthew 1:23

They shall call his name Emmanuel—To *be called*, only means, according to the Hebrew manner of speaking, that the person spoken of shall really and effectually be what He is called, and actually fulfill that title. Thus, *Unto us a child is born—and his name shall be called Wonderful, Counsellor, the Mighty God, the Prince of Peace*—That is, He shall be all these, though not so much nominally [by name], as really, and in effect. And thus was He called *Emmanuel*; which was no common name of Christ, but points out His nature and office; as He is God incarnate, and dwells by His Spirit in the hearts of His people.

It is observable, the words in Isaiah are, *Thou* (namely, His mother) *shalt call;* but here, *They*—that is, all His people, *shall call*— shall acknowledge *Him* to be Emmanuel, God with us. (ENNT)

Joseph Obeyed God's Instructions (Matt. 1:24–25)

Joseph's righteous nature was confirmed by his response to the dream from God: **He did what the angel of the Lord had commanded him and took Mary home as his wife** (v. 24). Joseph's great soul, which loved God and His word passionately, was willing to accept the gossip of the village and the damage to his own honorable reputation. For villagers would assume that in marrying Mary he was showing that he was in fact the father of Jesus, since no one in his right mind would marry a fiancée who had been impregnated by someone else. But obedience to God was more important to him than his reputation.

WORDS FROM WESLEY

Matthew 1:25: "Fruit of a Virgin's Womb"

The solemn hour is come
For God made visible,
Fruit of a virgin's womb,
A man with men to dwell;
The Saviour of the world to appear,
And found His heavenly kingdom here.
The sinner's Sacrifice,
The Head of angels see,
From Jesse's stem arise;
And grasp the Deity!
His sacred flesh the only shrine
That holds Immensity Divine.
Let all mankind abase
Their souls before the Lord,
And humbly prostrate, praise
The great incarnate Word,
And welcome Jesus from above,
With joy, and gratitude, and love. (PW, vol. 13, 257)

Matthew emphasized for us again the purely divine nature of the miraculous conception when he reported what followed. Not only did no human cause it, but even after marriage Joseph forfeited the privilege of marital relations with his wife (v. 25). His abstinence recognizes that something holy had taken place within Mary, and nothing would happen to question or profane the fleshly temple within which the mystery of the ages was taking place: God becoming man. Some Christians believe Mary continued to live as a virgin, though Joseph's wife, until her death. But the Bible gives no hint of this idea. If anything, the language of Matthew suggests that Mary was a virgin only until Jesus was born, and had a normal married life after that (as the existence of Jesus' brothers and sisters would imply; see Matt. 12:46–47; 13:55; John 7:3–5). The word of God through the angel was fulfilled when **she gave birth to a son**

(Matt. 1:25). God's promise is true; His hand worked the greatest miracle ever. **And he gave him the name Jesus** (v. 25); the naming expresses both obedience and hope. God's righteous servants Joseph and Mary responded in faith to share in the mysterious plan.

DISCUSSION

Emmanuel means "God with us"; and Christ is still present with us through the Holy Spirit.

1. What character qualities of Joseph are evident from these verses?

2. How might Joseph's reputation have been affected by his fiancée's condition?

3. Was Joseph's response to the news what you would have expected? Was Mary's? (See Luke 1:46–48.)

4. What more can we learn about this event from Luke 15:10?

5. If God asked you to believe the impossible, how do you think you would respond?

6. In what ways do our cultural Christmas traditions help to reinforce the news of Jesus' birth? In what ways do they detract from it?

7. List one way you can celebrate Jesus' birth every day.

8. Describe a time when you obeyed God when it didn't make sense.

9. What is one gift you have received from Jesus?

PRAYER

God, thank You for coming near to us in Emmanuel, Your Son. Help us to be mindful of Your closeness and Your salvation. Amen.

2

FINDING GOD ON THE BOTTOM SHELF

Matthew 5:1–12

God's blessing can be found in unlikely places.

How can you gain real security for your future? What makes people respect you? Where is the best place to find genuine acceptance? These days, the most likely answers to those questions could be (a) by making more money, (b) by achieving great success, and (c) from an Internet dating service. Those are some of the more obvious solutions provided by our culture.

But God's answers to life's big questions are almost always different than ours. While we may look in the most obvious places for love, security, and a sense of purpose, God generally provides these blessings in unlikely ways.

This study will lead you to reexamine your view of blessing and begin seeking God in some unexpected places.

COMMENTARY

Matthew focused on the kingdom of heaven, and Jesus directed the Sermon on the Mount to kingdom subjects. Who were these subjects? Matthew 5:1 provides a hint: The hearers are identified by physical proximity to Jesus. Closest are the disciples (kingdom subjects) and then the crowd (potential kingdom subjects).

The kingdom is the first blessing (5:3) and the last (vv. 10, 12). The Beatitudes may have been designed to whet the appetites of the unbelieving, but their greater message was to those who considered themselves kingdom citizens. Jesus said, "This is how to be happy under heaven."

The Source of Happiness, from Whom (Matt. 5:1–2)

It is tempting to skip over introductions and sink our teeth into the real meat. But remember who is in these verses. Jesus himself, the source of kingdom blessings, is providing instruction on how to be happy under heaven.

WORDS FROM WESLEY

Jesus and Hapiness

To bless men, to make men happy, was the great business for which our Lord came into the world. And accordingly He here pronounces eight blessings together, annexing them to so many steps in Christianity. Knowing that happiness is our common aim, and that an innate instinct continually urges us to the pursuit of it, He in the kindest manner applies to that instinct, and directs it to its proper object.

Though all men desire, yet few attain, happiness, because they seek it where it is not to be found. Our Lord therefore begins His divine institution, which is the complete art of happiness, by laying down before all that have ears to hear, the true and only true method of acquiring it.

Observe the benevolent condescension of our Lord. He seems, as it were, to lay aside His supreme authority as our legislator, that He may the better act the part of our friend and Saviour. Instead of using the lofty style, in positive commands, He in a more gentle and engaging way, insinuates His will and our duty, by pronouncing those happy who comply with it. (ENNT)

In the United States the attainment of happiness has historic status in "life, liberty, and the pursuit of happiness." It is a goal. Yet in Jesus we see happiness not as a goal, but as a result. Jesus came with a mission from His Father. He placed himself willingly under heaven. He lived verse 10; He lived all the Beatitudes.

Looking out on the **crowds**, Jesus **went up on a mountainside** (v. 1). We might have wanted an escape, but for Jesus the retreat was a staging area for greater advance, a marshaling of His forces for taking more ground. The Enemy had the throng under his confusing control, but the kingdom of heaven was at hand. Before Jesus milled a needy multitude of unhappy people seeking solace, He had the answer in himself. Most intimately to the **disciples**, who had taken their first wobbly kingdom steps, Jesus opened the heart of heaven. Tantalizingly before the crowds, He spoke words that contradicted life as they knew it and offered life as it could be. Jesus placed himself under heaven to offer us the kingdom.

The Condition for Happiness, from Within (Matt. 5:3–9)

Nine successive sentences begin with the word *blessed* (Greek, *makarioi*). The first seven form the kingdom character Christ promotes. One translation of the Bible uses *happy* at each point *makarioi* appears (GNB). *Blessed* tends to leave us in misty clouds; the world around us considers it quaint. *Happy* has its problems, as well. Both words tend to suggest an apathetic disconnect with surroundings that allows selfish satisfaction. The Christian engages with today's world. Kingdom subjects care about their neighbor's situation. *Happy* often is rejected for another reason: Some say happiness depends on circumstances, while blessedness does not. However, both depend on circumstances. What matters are the circumstances you depend on. The continuing kingdom circumstance is the presence of God Almighty. Due to that happy truth, we can allow Christ to develop in us attitudes reflecting a confidence in God's sovereignty.

The first seven groups of people described by Christ display attitudes of the heart that place them in a position to be blessed. Their blessing is both present and future. Their very attitude marks them as blessed now. Our present blessings reside in our proper expectation of God fulfilling His promises. Today that fulfillment is incremental; tomorrow will bring overflowing abundance. Heaven will offer in barrels what we now carry in buckets. Note, too, that these are not individuals, but rather like-minded groups: "Blessed are the" and "Blessed are those" who display certain attitudes and desires of the heart. The kingdom of heaven consists of voluntary subjects united under the rule and order of the King.

One danger of the Beatitudes stems from their elegant simplicity. Take one out, roll it around in the mind, even make it a memory verse; then set it aside where it can't bother any others. Taken individually, that happens easily; in context, it becomes more difficult. Together they form kingdom character—our proper Christian character. We may grow more at one point now and then, but we leave any out to our peril.

WORDS FROM WESLEY

Matthew 5:3

Happy are the poor—In the following discourse there is, 1. A sweet invitation to true holiness and happiness, ver. 3–12. 2. A persuasive to impart it to others, ver. 13–16. 3. A description of true Christian holiness, ver. 17–chap. 7:12 (in which it is easy to observe, the latter part exactly answers the former:) 4. The conclusion: giving a sure mark of the true way, warning against false prophets, exhorting to follow after holiness. *The poor in spirit*— They who are unfeignedly penitent, they who are truly convinced of sin; who see and feel the state they are in by nature, being deeply sensible of their sinfulness, guiltiness, helplessness. *For theirs is the kingdom of heaven*—The present inward kingdom: righteousness, and peace, and joy in the Holy Ghost, as well as the eternal kingdom, if they endure to the end. (ENNT)

Another danger derives from their contradictory element. Each runs counter to our expectations. The culture of the world has immunized us from kingdom cures. Give Christ's words time to make your life a contradiction to the ways of the world. Then you will be salt and light (Matt. 5:13–16).

Blessed are the poor in spirit, for theirs is the kingdom of heaven (v. 3). The poor in spirit know their continuing need of God. This places them in position to receive the blessing of His constant presence. That presence is the kingdom of heaven, now in the form of a gracious earnest deposit, later the whole payment. Certainly this poorness of spirit begins before salvation, but it does not end there. One cannot legitimately say, "Well, I was poor in spirit and repented, now I can get over it." Being poor in spirit is a kingdom characteristic that is an inner knowledge of ongoing need combined with gratitude for constant supply in God himself.

WORDS FROM WESLEY

Matthew 5:4–6

4. *They that mourn*—Either for their own sins, or for other men's, and are steadily and habitually serious. *They shall be comforted*—More solidly and deeply even in this world, and eternally in heaven.

5. *Happy are the meek*—They that hold all their passions and affections evenly balanced. *They shall inherit the earth*—They shall have all things really necessary for life and godliness. They shall *enjoy* whatever portion God hath given them here, and shall hereafter *possess* the new earth, wherein dwelleth righteousness.

6. *They that hunger and thirst after righteousness*—After the holiness here described. *They shall be satisfied* with it. (ENNT)

Blessed are those who mourn, for they will be comforted (v. 4). Those who mourn discern their dying state and God as their only hope. Who is not familiar with grief and mourning? Sometimes it sweeps down when least expected: an accident, a diagnosis, a tornado. Other times mourning comes as a growing realization: a progressive debilitation, an advancing enemy, a changing economy. Jesus knew that to be human is to be familiar with the deep sorrow of mourning loss. Blessedness and grief, happiness and mourning—can they go together? According to Christ they not only can, they must! But He is talking about deep agony of the soul: agony about our lostness without Him, about our darkened understanding even with Him, and about our lost and dying world. Jesus exhibited this last agony one day overlooking Jerusalem: "O Jerusalem, Jerusalem . . . how often I have longed to gather your children together, as a hen gathers her chicks under her wings, but you were not willing" (Matt. 23:37). Our present blessing comes as proper mourning sees God as the ultimate comfort.

Blessed are the meek, for they will inherit the earth (5:5). Being among the meek reflects our lofty position. Meekness comes when we trust God with our promised inheritance. Because we as Christians are adopted family, He is on record as disposed to act on our behalf. That is not a reason for arrogant pride; rather, a reason for gentle meekness. Because we are wrapped in His strong robes, we act gently with those who do not yet understand. The strength of the meek is evident in balanced response. Meekness is not weakness, for Christ used the term to describe himself. The same Greek word, *praus*, is translated *meek* in our beatitude, and *gentle* later in Matthew: "Take my yoke upon you and learn from me, for I am *gentle* and humble in heart" (11:29, emphasis added). Jesus did not become "unmeek" when He overturned the tables at the temple; He devised a response appropriate to the situation. Meekness pervaded His incarnation with its release of godly rights (see Phil. 2:5–11).

Blessed are those who hunger and thirst for righteousness, for they will be filled (Matt. 5:6). Satisfaction in God's kingdom requires a consuming desire for righteousness. This beatitude carries the seeds of blessing in the characteristic described. The desire may be contradictory, but within itself this one seems to make sense. Look at its simple power. Do you lack satisfaction in your walk with God? If you don't have a desire, it is not likely you will fulfill it. Could it be you don't have a desire for righteousness? The hard truth is if you are not satisfied, you are seeking the wrong thing.

WORDS FROM WESLEY

Matthew 5:6

Happy soul, whose active love
Emulates the bless'd above,
In thy every action seen,
Sparkling from the soul within:
Thou to every sufferer nigh,
Hearest, not in vain, the cry
Of the widow in distress,
Of the poor and fatherless!
Raiment thou to all that need,
To the hungry deal'st thy bread,
To the sick thou givest relief,
Soothest the hapless prisoner's grief,
The weak hands thou liftest up,
Bidd'st the helpless mourners hope,
Givest to those in darkness light,
Guidest the weary wanderer right,
Break'st the roaring lion's teeth,
Savest the sinner's soul from death;
Happy thou, for-God doth own
Thee, His well-beloved son. (PW, vol. 4, 321–22)

Blessed are the merciful, for they will be shown mercy (v. 7). Hebrews connects Christ's human experience with His capacity to be a "merciful and faithful high priest in service to God" (Heb. 2:17). This quality should appear in us because we have a shared experience with the world around us. It goes deeper: Kingdom mercy moves us to set aside our momentary needs for the needs of others. We are motivated especially to alleviate spiritual suffering, even when that suffering is earned. Certainly we are grateful God dealt with us this way. The associated kingdom blessing is the happy thought we also will be objects of kingdom mercy. We can happily delay our gratification knowing, once again, it is in good hands.

Blessed are the pure in heart, for they will see God (Matt. 5:8). The disciples and larger throng would recognize the word *pure* (Greek, *katharos*) as one associated with ritual cleansing. The one who was pure had followed outer washings and avoided defilement that came from touching a dead body or other happenings of everyday life. While not criticizing such lawful proscriptions, Christ deepened the concept to inward purity—an attitude that contains consistent, undiluted love for God culminating in godly behavior. What a bland blessing for the impure; what a frightening thought for the wicked; what more to seek for those pure in heart! Seeing God later requires seeing Him now.

WORDS FROM WESLEY
Matthew 5:7–9

7. *The merciful*—The tender-hearted: they who love all men as themselves: *They shall obtain mercy*—Whatever mercy therefore we desire from God, the same let us show to our brethren. He will repay us a thousand fold, the love we bear to any for His sake.

8. *The pure in heart*—The sanctified: they who love God with all their hearts. *They shall see God*—In all things here; hereafter in glory.

9. *The peace-makers*—They that out of love to God and man do all possible good to all men. *Peace* in the Scripture sense implies all blessings temporal and eternal. *They shall be called the children of God*—Shall be acknowledged such by God and man. One would imagine a person of this amiable temper and behaviour would be the darling of mankind. But our Lord well knew it would not be so, as long as Satan was the prince of this world. He therefore warns them before of the treatment all were to expect, who were determined thus to tread in His steps, by immediately subjoining, *Happy* are *they who* are *persecuted for righteousness' sake*. (ENNT)

Blessed are the peacemakers, for they will be called sons of God (v. 9). Christ came to end enmity between God and people, between one person and another, and between a person and him- or herself. To take up that ministry is to be honored with a title akin to our Savior's: children of God.

The Participation of Happiness, from Without (Matt. 5:10–12)

The former set of beatitudes dealt with inner realities. This latter beatitude and the next three verses deal with an outer reality. Persecution happens to kingdom subjects *because* of their inner character. A reasonable person concludes that treating others with loving respect results in a like response. Yet it is not always so. The clear message is that if you truly live with godly purpose and passion, you will not always get along with everyone. The cross of Christ is certainly a historical oddity if getting along and working with are the highest goals of kingdom living. The fact is, persecution will come with godly living.

WORDS FROM WESLEY

Matthew 5:10

Tonight I proceeded in the Beatitudes. When I came to the last, 'Blessed are they which are persecuted,' &c.; our enemies, not knowing the Scriptures, fulfilled them. A troop poured in from a neighbouring alehouse, and set up their champion, a schoolmaster, upon a bench over against me. For near an hour, he spake for his master, and I for mine; but my voice prevailed. Sometimes we prayed, sometimes sang and gave thanks. The Lord our God was with us, and the shout of a King was amongst us. In the midst of tumult, reproach, and blasphemy, I enjoyed a sweet calm within, even while I preached the Gospel with most contention. These slighter conflicts must fit me for greater. (LCW, vol. 1, 211)

Interestingly, this beatitude picks up the same reason for considering yourself blessed as in verse 3: **for theirs is the kingdom of heaven** (v. 10). Jesus seemed to have a reason for the repetition: to combine all kingdom characteristics to be displayed in this world. Kingdom subjects have Beatitude attitudes. These attitudes are essential to successfully impact a hostile world. Jesus reiterated the persecution point with another **blessed** (v. 11), but this time He replaced **because of righteousness** (v. 10) with

because of me. In the kingdom of heaven, loyalty to Jesus is loyalty to righteousness and vice versa. The kingdom was before them bodily in the person of Jesus. Jesus brings the kingdom of heaven to us as well. Our happiness, **rejoice and be glad** (v. 12), is a present happiness based on past history (**persecuted the prophets who were before you**) and future reward (**great is your reward in heaven**).

Happiness under heaven depends on keeping yourself ever under God and in the presence of His Spirit. Seeing Jesus as your most significant circumstance will help you choose joy in the most trying times. Neither the disciples nor the crowds knew it then, but not only did they have an opportunity to share in the fate of the prophets, they also were to share the fate of Jesus himself. On this side of the cross we surely know it. Be glad.

DISCUSSION

The Beatitudes describe the truly blessed, richly satisfied life of one whose life has been transformed.

1. To whom did Jesus give this teaching? Who else was present? What differences in understanding do you think might have characterized those groups of people?

2. In what ways was Jesus' teaching different than that of the law? In what ways was it the same?

3. Do you agree with the statement "meekness is controlled strength"? Why or why not?

4. How would you define *holy discontent*?

5. Which grieves you more: seeing sin in your life or losing something you love? Why do you think that's the case?

6. Tell about a time God comforted you when you lost something or someone very dear.

7. Do you think spiritual hunger is ever fully satisfied? Why or why not?

8. In what ways do you try to satisfy your hunger for God? Which are most effective?

9. In what ways might the church change if we all lived according to the Sermon on the Mount?

PRAYER

Father, help us to understand and live what Jesus taught. Amen.

AVOIDING SPIRITUAL PRIDE

Matthew 6:1–18

We practice spiritual disciplines in order to please God,
not to impress others.

W hat does a religious person look like? Often, those who have
had a good deal of religious training will answer that question by
looking in the mirror. We know habits of spirituality and the
activities of worship, and we can't help but be pleased by the
way we exemplify goodness.

Sadly, it is all too easy for us to begin practicing these laudable
acts of piety for the wrong audience. Rather than praying, tithing, or
serving others to please God and grow in humility, we may begin to
do these things to impress others, giving pride a foothold in our lives.

This study will challenge you to consider the motive behind
the good things you do and to direct your attention to the only
audience that matters—God.

COMMENTARY

In this section of the Sermon on the Mount, Jesus tackled three
traditional forms of Jewish devotion to God: charity, prayer, and
fasting.

He repeated a certain pattern three times in this section. First,
the type of behavior was named, and then the disciples were urged
not to perform it in order to be seen and honored by society (as
"hypocrites"). Those who did, Jesus warned, had already received
their reward. Then Jesus described the right way to demonstrate
devotion to God. We can conclude that these are important
principles, since our Lord emphasized them by repetition.

Right Worship Part 1: On Charity (Matt. 6:1–4)

This section is introduced with a general admonition: **Be careful not to do your "acts of righteousness" before men, to be seen by them** (v. 1). **Acts of righteousness** is probably a general term for any pious deed.

What is wrong with doing something to be seen? After all, didn't Jesus himself tell us in this same sermon to "let your light shine before men, that they may see your good deeds and praise your Father in heaven" (5:16)? The difference lies in who gets the praise. In chapter 5, God received the glory. Here in chapter 6, the person is performing "acts of righteousness" to honor him- or herself.

In first-century Palestine, to be thought of as a pious person was sure to boost your reputation among your neighbors. People desired honor and status as much or more than wealth. Even today, politicians may use churchgoing to raise their standing in opinion polls. And within our local churches, we (rightly) respect and seek the advice of those who have a reputation for being pious. It is very tempting to want that sort of attention, or even to attempt to enhance our reputation by making sure others notice how spiritual we are. But once we begin to do this, we are no longer pursuing God.

The judgment on "hypocrites" is that **you will have no reward from your Father in heaven** (6:1). The idea of reward from God for the righteous is an important theme in Jesus' teaching. Some scholars are not comfortable talking about a reward from God, arguing that we descend into viewing morality as buying favors from God. Scripture, however, teaches that our Creator is not stingy, but rather delights to reward those who love Him.

Next, Jesus took up a specific example of "doing righteousness." **When you give to the needy** (v. 2) could also be translated "Whenever you do a 'mercy,'" because charity is thought of as imitating the generosity and mercy God shows to us daily. We echo His character when we share with those in need. Jesus assumed giving would be typical behavior for His followers. This is why He said "when," not "if" you give to the needy. This is a good reminder that to be righteous does not only mean abstaining from evil, but includes taking positive action to benefit others.

WORDS FROM WESLEY

Matthew 6:1

In the preceding chapter our Lord has described inward religion in its various branches. He has laid before us those dispositions of soul which constitute real Christianity; the inward tempers contained in that "holiness, without which no man shall see the Lord;" the affections which, when flowing from their proper fountain, from a living faith in God through Christ Jesus, are intrinsically and essentially good, and acceptable to God. He proceeds to show, in this chapter, how all our actions likewise, even those that are indifferent in their own nature, may be made holy, and good, and acceptable to God, by a pure and holy intention. Whatever is done without this, He largely declares, is of no value before God. Whereas, whatever outward works are thus consecrated to God, they are, in His sight, of great price. (WJW, vol. 5, 328)

Jesus was fond of dramatic images that made His words easy to remember. Who can forget the image of self-important egotists blowing **trumpets** (v. 2), usually used only to announce special holy days or as a general alarm for war, as they drop a few coins into the poor box or a beggar's lap?

The word *hypocrite* originally referred to an actor in a Greek drama. In Jesus' teaching, the hypocrite (v. 2) is someone who acts pious in front of people in order to win attention, honor, and praise. This person has no real relationship with God but rather uses God to get something else.

The verb Matthew used for **they have received** (v. 2) has been found in papyrus documents from ancient Egypt. It comes from the commercial world of business. Papyrus tax receipts, records of loans being paid off, and other documents that record payment of a debt have this same word scrawled across the bottom. It means that as far as God is concerned, hypocrites who do their spiritual exercises to be well thought of have received (from people) all the reward they will ever get. God owes them nothing.

Instead, Jesus urged His followers to **not let your left hand know what your right hand is doing** (v. 3), which is to say godly charity should be done unobtrusively, keeping it to yourself as much as possible. This is to serve God **in secret** (v. 4).

Right Worship Part 2: On Prayer (Matt. 6:5–15)

The same pattern of teaching we saw with charity is repeated with prayer: We are not to be like **hypocrites** (v. 5), who use prayer to draw attention to themselves and boost their reputations. Standing was a normal position for prayer, but the hypocrite loves to pray where he or she will be seen—as at a major crossroads. Instead, we are instructed: **When you pray, go into your room, close the door and pray** (v. 6). This way we cannot gain anything from people for our spirituality; we are focused solely on God. In addition, we are cautioned not to be like **pagans** (v. 7), a term originally referring to non-Jews, people who do not have God's revelation. Their error is that **they think they will be heard because of their many words**, and hence—perhaps to get God's attention by nagging Him, or perhaps by repeating senseless syllables they believe have magical power—they **keep on babbling**.

God is perfectly intelligent, and should be spoken to in accordance with His dignity. He already **knows what you need before you ask** (v. 8). So our prayers can be simple and to the point. This is also a matter of trust. Jesus asks us to regard God as our **Father**, who loves and cares for us (vv. 8–9).

WORDS FROM WESLEY

Matthew 6:8

Your Father knoweth what things ye have need of—We do not pray to inform God of our wants. Omniscient as He is, He cannot be informed of any thing which He knew not before: and He is always willing to relieve them. The chief thing wanting is, a fit disposition on our part to receive His grace and blessing. Consequently, one great office of prayer is, to produce such a disposition in us: to exercise our dependence on God; to increase our desire of the things we ask for; to make us so sensible of our wants, that we may never cease wrestling till we have prevailed for the blessing. (ENNT)

Using our minds to form prayer is good, even encouraged by Jesus, as long as prayer does not become an occasion to parade our skills in front of others. But our thoughts need guidance, so Jesus provided His disciples (and us) a prayer that is both good to pray by itself and a guide to prayer in general.

First, God is addressed as **our Father in heaven** (v. 9). It was extremely rare in Jesus' day for anyone to call God **Father** in prayer. And no one would have dared use the informal term Jesus commonly used for God: Aramaic *Abba*, which is a child's word meaning *daddy*. **Father** stresses His role as creator and life-giver, as the One who provides for us, loves, teaches, punishes, and rewards us. In Jesus' world, **Father** also strongly suggested God's authority over us, and the honor He is due.

Hallowed be your name (v. 9) is a prayer that the world show "reverence" to God (**your name** may refer to God himself or to His reputation). To "hallow" is to sanctify, or treat as holy. This honoring of God's name will happen completely and ultimately when His kingdom comes in fullness and every knee bows to the Son as Lord, to God's glory (Phil. 2:10–11). Hence the first three petitions in this prayer are tied together, nearly identical in meaning.

Your kingdom come (Matt. 6:10) asks God to bring His universal rule in a final and triumphant way to earth, to end all wickedness and suffering, to restore the earth and His faithful people to their "pre-fall" condition, and to grant eternal life to His saints. The kingdom of God was the central theme of Jesus' teaching. He called people to repent and be ready to enter it, and sent His disciples out to preach the same. And finally He died and rose from the dead so we might receive the blessings of the kingdom. The word *kingdom* could also mean God's rule as king; and so **your will be done** (v. 10) could be one definition of God's kingdom coming.

Humans can choose whether to enter into God's plans and God's blessings. In the Lord's Prayer, we not only ask that God be honored and obeyed by *others*, but we ask that *we ourselves* obey and share in His work, with His help. **As it is in heaven** (v. 10) gives a dramatic picture of what we are asking: that God make earth like heaven, fully submitted to Him.

The one petition for physical needs is for **bread** (v. 11), a staple of ancient Palestinian diets. **Bread** also stands for food in general. Most likely this is a real request for food to sustain life. God is celebrated in the Old Testament as the One who gave grain and other food to Israel (see Gen. 27:28; Ps. 65:9; Joel 2:19). We too trust Him as creator and provider.

Forgive us our debts, as we also have forgiven our debtors (Matt. 6:12). Forgiveness is a necessary foundation to any right relationship with God. It presumes two things: (1) We have done wrong against God and people; and (2) we are offered the opportunity to repent. Notice Jesus does not teach us to pray "*if* we have sinned," because He knows we have. "Debt" is a very Jewish way of referring to sin: We owe God something (right living and worship) that we have not paid.

Some people are unsure of the expression **as we also have forgiven**, worried that it endangers the biblical doctrine of God's grace if we believe His forgiveness rests on our forgiving others first. But verses 14–15 clearly teach that if we refuse to exercise the grace of forgiveness to others, God will deprive us of His forgiveness. It is not that we "earn" God's favor by forgiving. Rather, His children risk His wrath if they refuse to offer to others the same grace they themselves received.

WORDS FROM WESLEY

Matthew 6:1–18

Jesus, if Thou Thy servant guard,
I shall obey Thy laws,
Nor seek from man my base reward,
Nor aim at his applause:
O may I cast the world behind,
While in Thy work employ'd,
And only bear it in my mind
That I am seen of God.
Through false pretence of honouring Thee
Whoe'er themselves proclaim
Indulge their secret vanity,
And cloak it with Thy name;
For all their works and righteousness,
The hypocrites abhorr'd
In human, momentary praise
Receive their whole reward.
Lord, Thou know'st, I would be seen
Doing good by foolish men,
Nature still usurps a part,
More than shares with Thee my heart:
Jesus, set my nature right,
Shut the creature from my sight,
Thou mine only Object be,
More than all the world to me.
Father, create my heart again,
That dead to the esteem of men,
Contentedly unknown,
In all I think, or speak, or do,
I humbly may the praise pursue
Which comes from God alone. (PW, vol. 10, 174, 175, 186)

Lead us not into temptation (v. 13) is one of the hardest phrases to interpret here, for we do not imagine God tempting people to do evil. In fact, James asserts plainly that we must not blame God for our temptation (James 1:13). The solution may be found in the fact that the word translated *temptation* (Greek, *peirasmos*) also means a "testing." This is a prayer for spiritual humility. Abraham was tested; Jesus was tested in the wilderness. But we don't want to be tested ourselves. We are invited to think of ourselves as those who are "poor in spirit" (Matt. 5:3), utterly dependent on God. Hence, instead of boasting about our spiritual strength, we ask, **deliver us from the evil one** (6:13).

God as creator is ultimately in control of everything in the universe, including supernatural beings. To be delivered from Satan is not the same as being delivered from every physical evil, for saints of God who live in faith get sick, have accidents, experience persecution, and eventually die. We are requesting that we not be swayed by evil's appeal, nor by the lies Satan spreads by way of our culture. To have our hearts made captive by Satan would mean being cut off from God for eternity.

Right Worship Part 3: On Fasting (Matt. 6:16–18)

The final religious practice Jesus mentioned is fasting, going without food to devote oneself to prayer and meditation on God and His Word. Here again it is worth noting that Jesus assumed it will be done ("when" not "if"). There are different types of fasting both then and now. Some people fasted only during the daytime and ate a meal after sundown; others gave up food entirely for a period of time. Jesus does not criticize fasting in itself, but doing it to receive attention and honor from people. So His disciples were urged to hide the fact they were fasting by acting and dressing normally. It becomes something done "secretly" for God alone.

DISCUSSION

Holiness goes beyond our outward actions to the inward transformation of our hearts.

1. What prompted Jesus to teach on the subject of prayer? Do you think the circumstances shaped His response? Why or why not?

2. Is Jesus saying we should never pray in public? Explain your answer.

3. Since God knows what we need before we ask, why should we bother to bring requests to Him?

4. If God measured out only what we gave to others in the area of mercy or judgment, what would be the portion?

5. When a Christian is in the spotlight, is he or she in the wrong? Explain.

6. What does it mean to role-play before God?

7. How would you explain the difference between the "applause" from heaven and the applause of men?

8. Describe what it would feel like to go to heaven and discover all your rewards were received on earth.

9. Would you still serve if no one ever applauded, acknowledged, or saw your work?

10. Name ways you could bless someone in secret.

PRAYER

Father, purify our hearts today. May all we do be for Your honor and glory alone. Amen.

4

FIRST THINGS FIRST

Matthew 6:19–34

When we seek God's priorities, we receive God's provisions.

Stress is a fact of life for just about everyone. And no activity brings on stress more quickly than a discussion of finances. We worry about making mortgage payments, scraping together money for college, and finding the safest or most profitable place to invest for retirement. From corporate offices to living rooms to church boardrooms, tempers rise and impassioned speeches abound when money is the topic of the hour. That should never be the case, according to Jesus. Faith should always be our first concern; money will always be subordinate to that.

This study will help to relieve the stress we often feel about finances and help us relax in the care of our heavenly Father.

COMMENTARY

These verses come from the heart of the Sermon on the Mount, the longest and best-known record of Jesus' teaching. In this passage, Jesus described life in the kingdom of God. When Jesus came, God's kingly rule or authority came into the world in a new way. Jesus delivered people from sin and from bondage to the Devil. He called people to submit to God's rule and receive this deliverance. Those who submitted were set free from their sin and brought into a new relationship with God. By God's grace they were able to live a new kind of life.

The Beatitudes (Matt. 5:1–12) introduce the sermon by describing those who enter God's kingdom. Such people realize they are utterly destitute before God. God blesses the people who come to Him in this way by giving them the new life of the kingdom. This new life enables them to live according to the instructions given in the rest of the Sermon on the Mount.

Matthew 5:13–16 makes it clear that the people described in the Beatitudes are to live out their discipleship in the world. Others will see the new life they live and come to believe in Christ. But what will this new life look like? It will be greater and deeper than life lived by a legalistic keeping of the Mosaic law. Verses 17–20 make this fact quite clear. Life in the kingdom is not a life based on rule keeping. It is based on true inner transformation. According to Jesus, this kind of life fulfills the true meaning of the Old Testament law.

In Matthew 5:21–48, Jesus gave a series of contrasts between life based on keeping the letter of the Mosaic law and life based on the inner transformation of the kingdom. These contrasts describe how this inner transformation affects our relationship to others. In each contrast Jesus introduced life according to the letter of the law by "You have heard that it was said" or "It was said." Life based on inner transformation by God's grace is introduced by "But I tell you." Jesus is the one who gives the true meaning of the law.

In Matthew 6:1–34, Jesus showed how the inner transforming power of the kingdom transforms our relationship with God. How does life in the kingdom transform our pursuit of prestige, material wealth, and security? The person of the kingdom seeks God's approval, not human acclaim (6:1–18). The person of the kingdom seeks for God's will to be done and His kingdom to be established rather than for material possessions and pleasures of this life (6:19–34).

The study passage focuses on the competing claims of possessions with their unstable security and the kingdom of God that is eternal. We are invited to enter God's kingdom by trusting

Him for the things of this world and setting our hearts wholly on doing and promoting His will.

Where Is Your Treasure? (Matt. 6:19–24)

In verses 19–24, Jesus painted three pictures—stored treasure, the eye of the body, and two masters. What is the message of these verses? Give yourself fully to God's kingdom rather than to the pursuit of material security. The **heart** (v. 21) and the **eye** (vv. 22–23) represent who we really are, the true nature of our real selves. Who will be the **master** (v. 24) of that true "me"?

The first picture is one of stored treasure (vv. 19–21). **Do not store up for yourselves treasures on earth.... But store up for yourselves treasures in heaven** (vv. 19–20). The first of these commands is clear: Don't spend your life accumulating material goods. But how do we store up treasures in heaven? By setting our hearts on and directing our actions toward doing God's will as zealously as others set their attention on material accumulation. Why should we accept Jesus' invitation to do this? Treasure on earth is really so unstable! The **moth and rust** (v. 20) of the stock market can **destroy** it in a moment. No amount of insurance will protect it. **Thieves** can swindle us out of it. Treasure in heaven is absolutely secure from all of these things. There is a dual relationship between our **treasure** and our **heart** (v. 21). If our hearts are set on the things of earth, we will amass earthly treasure, if on the things of heaven, heavenly treasure. But also, if we have been storing up treasure in heaven, our hearts will be on heaven. We will think about and give our efforts toward the place **where** our **treasure is**. No one knows exactly what the heavenly treasure looks like—"No eye has seen, no ear has heard, no mind has conceived what God has prepared for those who love him" (1 Cor. 2:9).

The second picture (Matt. 6:22–23) is the picture of the eye and the body. The physical **eye is the lamp of the body** (v. 22). The eye enables the body to perceive light, to see, and thus to direct life properly. Thus, if a person's **eyes are good** or "healthy" (NRSV), then that person's **whole body will be full of light**. He or she will be able to see, to understand what is around, and to live accordingly. On the other hand, if a person's eyes are "unhealthy" (**bad**), that person won't be able to see. He or she won't be able to conduct his or her life properly. Our eyes in this picture are equivalent to our hearts in the treasure picture. Our eyes are our true selves. If we have fixed our spiritual gaze on the kingdom of God, then our whole lives are full of light. We can live as God would have us live. But if not, then our whole lives are **full of darkness** (v. 23). Without God's kingdom, **how great is that darkness**!

WORDS FROM WESLEY

Matthew 6:19–23

And without question, the same purity of intention, "which makes our alms and devotions acceptable, must also make our labour or employment a proper offering to God. If a man pursues his business, that he may raise himself to a state of figure and riches in the world, he is no longer serving God in his employment, and has no more title to a reward from God, than he who gives alms that he may be seen, or prays that he may be heard, of men. For vain and earthly designs are no more allowable in our employments, than in our alms and devotions. They are not only evil when they mix with our good works," with our religious actions, "but they have the same evil nature when they enter into the common business of our employments. If it were allowable to pursue them in our worldly employments, it would be allowable to pursue them in our devotions. But as our alms and devotions are not an acceptable service but when they proceed from a pure intention, so our common employment cannot be reckoned a service to him but when it is performed with the same piety of heart." (WJW, vol. 5, 361–362)

The final picture brings out the significance of the previous two. No person can **serve** (v. 24)—that is, give total allegiance to—**two masters**. The images of **hate** and **love** and **be devoted** and **despise** express this truth in the strongest way. To serve two masters would be like playing on two opposing football teams or fighting in two opposing armies. One master will take precedence over the other. A person cannot be devoted both to **God** and to **Money**. The word the NIV's "money" can better be translated "wealth" (NRSV, NASB). It refers to all of the material benefits and enjoyments of this world. If our lives are focused on obtaining the things of this world, then we cannot truly serve God. How this temptation ensnares us! How easy to give up a six-figure profession to enter Christian service, and then be obsessed with getting a forty-thousand-dollar pastorate.

But how can we allow God to be first in our lives? How can we make His kingdom, His rule on earth, our first priority? After all, we need money to live. We have to have food. We need clothes. The next section of our study answers this question. We can trust the God we serve. He will take care of us.

Your Father Cares for You! (Matt. 6:25–34)

Jesus has told us that the things of this life are not to be our goal. Now He assures us that we don't even have to worry about them! Jesus doesn't mean we should become lazy. We are to work to provide for our needs. But He commands us: **Do not worry about your life, what you will eat** to preserve it; **or about your body, what you will wear** to cover it (v. 25). God cares for you and will supply. He has already given you the most important thing—your life. Will He not give you the food to sustain it? He has already given you a marvelous body; will He not provide the clothes necessary to cover it?

Jesus gave us two illustrations of God's care: The **birds of the air** (v. 26) give us a perfect example of how God will provide our food; the **lilies of the field** (v. 28) demonstrate God's provision of clothes.

Birds don't **sow, reap**, or **store** food (v. 26). They don't grow it, process it, or distribute it, yet God feeds them. Since He is **your heavenly Father**, you are much more important to Him than all the birds in the world. We can worry all we want to about getting the things of this life, but all our worrying won't **add a single hour to** our lives (v. 27).

Worry about clothes (v. 28)? How ridiculous! Nobody cultivates the **lilies of the field**; they are wildflowers. But look at them. **They do not labor or spin**. They don't grow cotton, make thread, weave cloth, or sew clothes. Yet their blossoms are more beautiful than **even Solomon in all his splendor** (v. 29). Second Chronicles 9:13–28 describes the fantastic wealth and majesty of Solomon's court. His legendary splendor was greater than that of any other Israelite king. Yet his finest clothes could not compare to the glory of a wildflower. God does this for **the grass of the field** (Matt. 6:30), which lives only for a moment. In wood-poor Palestine, grass was dried and used for fuel. How much more will God care for you, His children? Certainly He will **clothe you**. These two examples show both God's ability and God's care. When we worry about food and clothes and run after them, we don't trust our heavenly Father's care. We deserve to be addressed as **you of little faith** (v. 30).

Verses 31–33 summarize Jesus' point. Verse 31 gives a prohibition, followed by the reason for the prohibition in verse 32. Verse 33 gives Jesus' admonition, followed by the reason for His admonition.

First, the prohibition: **Do not worry, saying, "What shall we eat ... drink ... wear?"** (v. 31). Can you see the picture of people scurrying around seeking food, drink, and clothes? No need! Don't do it! If you do, you are acting like **the pagans** (v. 32). Pagans are those who don't know God as their loving **heavenly Father.** Certainly the heavenly Father can and will care for His children's earthly needs.

WORDS FROM WESLEY

Matthew 6:31

Therefore take not thought—How kind are these precepts! The substance of which is only this, Do thyself no harm! Let us not be so ungrateful to him, nor so injurious to ourselves, as to harass and oppress our minds with that burden of anxiety, which he has so graciously taken off. Every verse speaks at once to the understanding, and to the heart. We will not therefore indulge these unnecessary, these useless, these mischievous cares. We will not borrow the anxieties and distresses of the morrow, to aggravate those of the present day. Rather we will cheerfully repose ourselves on that heavenly Father, who knows we have need of these things: who has given us the life, which is more than meat, and the body, which is more than raiment. And thus instructed in the philosophy of our heavenly Master, we will learn a lesson of faith and cheerfulness, from every bird of the air, and every flower of the field. (ENNT)

So, **seek first his kingdom and his righteousness** (v. 33). We are reminded of the opening lines of the Lord's Prayer. Those who pray to "Our Father in heaven" also pray "your kingdom come, your will be done." When we know God as our heavenly Father, we give our lives to promoting His kingly rule on earth and to doing His will. Those who love the heavenly Father live to please Him. And when they love the Father, He takes care of them: **All these things will be given to you as well** (v. 33). What are **all these things**? The food and clothes that others so feverishly seek. Of course Jesus doesn't mean the Father will make all of His children wealthy. He will care for our needs and do what is best for us. Ultimately He will bring us into His eternal kingdom where suffering will be no more. But the important thing now, whether we have little or much, is to trust Him.

Verse 33 is the climax of Jesus' teaching on this subject, a verse well worth memorizing. We should say it to ourselves and give heed to it every time advertisements bombard us with our "need" for something more.

Verse 34 is a parting shot at worry. Like verse 27, it shows us the complete futility of being anxious over the future. Don't **worry about tomorrow**, because if you do you are just borrowing trouble. You don't even know what tomorrow's troubles will be, and you can't do anything about them anyway. Since we can't really deal with the future, how blessed we are to have a heavenly Father who can and will.

WORDS FROM WESLEY

Matthew 6:33–34

33. *Seek the kingdom of God and his righteousness*—Singly aim at this, that God reigning in your heart, may fill it with the righteousness above described. And indeed whosoever seeks this first, will soon come to seek this only.

34. *The morrow shall take thought for itself*—That is, be careful for the morrow when it comes. *The evil thereof*—Speaking after the manner of men: but all trouble is, upon the whole, a real good. It is good physic which God dispenses daily to his children, according to the need and the strength of each. (ENNT)

DISCUSSION

The person who trusts in Christ does not live in a world of scarcity but abundance.

1. Summarize Jesus' teaching on money.

2. Summarize Jesus' teaching on worry.

3. Do you agree or disagree that Jesus was telling His listeners to be lazy? Explain your view.

4. What factors in Jesus' day may have made this teaching hard for people to accept? What factors in our day may cause people to balk at it?

5. In Jesus' view, it is futile to try to control our lives. Which aspects of your life do you seem powerless to control?

6. How do you know when your life is out of control?

7. We are commanded to take one day of rest each week, yet people seldom do. Why do you suppose that is?

8. If you came to the end of your life suddenly, would you regret or celebrate the investment of your efforts?

9. How does seeking God bring balance to all areas of your life?

PRAYER

Lord, help us to enjoy Your gifts but hold them loosely. May we never forget their source in Your love and mercy. Amen.

5

EVIDENCE OF TRUE FAITH

Matthew 7:13–27

Our faith in Christ will be demonstrated by our obedience to Him.

Are we saved by what we believe or by what we do? Scholars and theologians on both sides of the question can marshal biblical support for their views.

Jesus' view is profound and practical, and it undercuts much of the wrangling that takes place on this question. To Christ, the answer is both. We are saved by faith in Christ; yet that faith, if genuine, will certainly be expressed in our daily choices. While there may be dividing lines between denominations, there can never be a divide between faith and action—they are inextricably linked.

This study will motivate you to go beyond seeing faith as a matter of the mind or even the heart to demonstrating faith through the choices you make.

COMMENTARY

When a new president of the United States enters office, he gives a speech that outlines the goals of his administration. Could we see the Sermon on the Mount as Jesus' inauguration address? In Matthew's account, this sermon comes early in Jesus' public ministry. From 4:12 through the end of that chapter, Matthew records Jesus' first words and acts among the people. He began to gather His "cabinet" (the apostles) around Him. Chapter 4 ends and chapter 5 begins with the mention of crowds. Jesus had quickly gathered a following. It's almost as if the people wanted Jesus to be their president.

But in this "inauguration address," Jesus did not emphasize His commitments to do great things for the nation. He focused, instead, on what He expected from people who follow Him. His true disciples did not tag along merely to see more spectacular miracles. The sermon as a whole lays out the "cost of discipleship." Jesus called the people to enter a lifestyle that contrasts greatly with that of contemporary society.

Throughout this sermon, note the theme of contrast between the disciples of Jesus and those who live around them.

The Beatitudes (5:1–12) praise character traits most people avoid, such as poverty, grief, and hunger. The next verses call true disciples to stick out in a crowd: Be salt and light (5:13–16). The next big block describes the disciples' relation to the Old Testament law (5:17–48). Are Jesus' people to discard their spiritual heritage? No, He calls them to take the law *even more seriously* than other Jews. By internalizing the law, Jesus' disciples would become even more righteous than the Pharisees. In the next chunk of the sermon (6:1–18), Jesus contrasted His followers with hypocrites (6:2, 5, 16), who do right things for wrong reasons. Then, when it comes to material possessions, Christ's disciples would not worry as the world did; Jesus called them to trust God their Father (6:19–34). The Golden Rule summarizes the first part of chapter 7. As disciples don't wish to be condemned, they do not condemn. Instead they pray, asking God to bless others and care for themselves (7:7–12). From the beginning of the sermon to its end, Jesus described how the lives of true disciples contrast with the lives of others, even other religious people, around them.

The passage for this study comprises the last fifteen verses of Jesus' sermon. Just as the sermon body highlighted contrast after contrast, so does the sermon conclusion. He calls His people to respond, to become true disciples, by pointing out contrasts between those who heed His call and those who reject it. Note the pattern.

Before looking at these contrasts individually, notice one feature all four share. In each case, Jesus lays out only two alternatives. People could choose to follow Him, or if they did not, they moved themselves toward destruction (v. 13), the fire (v. 19), away from the kingdom of heaven (v. 23), and a great crash (v. 27). Jesus graphically portrayed the results of disobedience in hopes that more people would follow Him.

The Two Gates (Matt. 7:13–14)

The sermon conclusion's first contrast pictures a wide gate leading to a wide road. For those who enjoy hiking, some days you want to relax, so you take a broad, level trail that you could almost walk with your eyes closed. Other days, you want a challenge, so you find a difficult, narrow trail that requires hard work to reach the end. Jesus said that following Him involves entering a narrow gate and walking a hard path. As we think back through the Sermon on the Mount, we can see what He meant. Anyone, with *no effort whatsoever*, can live in anger (5:22), lust (5:28), pride (6:1), or worry (6:25). **Many** (7:13) people travel that route. The crowds naturally go with the flow. Even as He spoke these words, Jesus addressed a large crowd. He held no false hope that all would become His disciples. That would require that people drop all the baggage of sin they carried (see Heb. 12:1), so they could fit through the narrow gate, ready for the challenge of climbing the narrow difficult path.

The two paths (and there are only two!) lead to different destinations. The easiest paths head downhill. The slope makes the walking easier. None of us know all the details of hell, but is it any wonder that we have always seen it as a downward destination? "Make your choice," Jesus said, "but remember that the path you choose determines where you go."

WORDS FROM WESLEY

The Two Gates and Two Trees

Our Lord, having warned us of the dangers which easily beset us at our first entrance upon real religion, the hinderances which naturally arise from within, from the wickedness of our own hearts; now proceeds to apprize us of the hinderances from without, particularly ill example and ill advice. By one or the other of these, thousands, who once ran well, have drawn back unto perdition;—yea, many of those who were not novices in religion, who had made some progress in righteousness. His caution, therefore, against these He presses upon us with all possible earnestness, and repeats again and again, in variety of expressions, lest by any means we should let it slip. Thus, effectually to guard us against the former, "Enter ye in," saith He, "at the strait gate: For wide is the gate, and broad is the way, that leadeth to destruction, and many there be which go in thereat: Because strait is the gate, and narrow is the way, which leadeth unto life, and few there be that find it:" To secure us from the latter, "Beware," saith He, "of false prophets." (WJW, vol. 5, 405)

The Two Trees (Matt. 7:15–20)

In the first paragraph of His sermon conclusion, Jesus drew two large contrasts, but the two include many smaller contrasts (two gates, paths, degrees of difficulty, and destinations). His second paragraph also includes a major contrast that includes sub-contrasts.

Jesus only implied the first sub-contrast. He spoke of the false prophet, but did not here specifically mention any true prophets. He did not need to; Jesus stood before them as the truth itself. But Jesus knew that even those who chose to walk the narrow trail would continually hear voices calling them down to more comfortable paths. False prophets would announce that many paths lead to the same heavenly destination. False prophets would proclaim that if you thought you were following Jesus, if you thought He had forgiven your sins, you could live any way you wanted. But Jesus had himself spoken true prophecy: There are only two ways and only one of them leads to life.

The false prophet often pretends to be a true sheep, but he is not from the flock. He is a savage wolf that can destroy the flock. As John Stott wrote in *The Message of the Sermon on the Mount*, such prophets are both "deceptive and dangerous."

Deceptive? They knowingly lead people astray, pretending to speak the truth. (The wolf did not just happen to wake up one morning wearing a sheepskin.) Dangerous? The false prophets offer teaching that, when followed, leads to destruction.

WORDS FROM WESLEY

Matthew 7:20

Must we not then with patience wait,
False to distinguish from sincere?
Or can we on another's state
Pronounce, *before* the fruits appear?
Can we the witnesses receive
Who of their own perfection boast,
The fairest words as fruit receive?
The fairest words are leaves at most.
How shall we then the spirits prove?
Their actions with their words compare,
And wait—till humblest meekest love
Their perfect nothingness declare:
But if the smallest spark of pride,
Or selfishness, break out at last,
Set the false-witnesses aside;
Yet hold the truth for ever fast. (PW, vol. 10, 203)

How can we sense whether a particular prophet is a harmless member of our sheep family or a wolf out to attack? Jesus changed His analogy to answer that question. He moved from zoology to horticulture, from farm animals to the farm orchard. He invited His followers to watch the trees to see the fruit they bore. It doesn't take a rocket scientist to detect that a tree that produces apples must be an apple tree. A tree that produces Jesus-like fruit must be a

Jesus-like tree. Time not only reveals a tree's species; it demonstrates its quality. Trees that produces no fruit at all waste space. The farmer quickly cuts out those trees to give space to fruit-bearing trees. What was Jesus saying? Be wary of the people who say it does not matter how you live. In time, you will see that in their character and conduct, they are not bearing Jesus fruit, or anything close. Those trees/prophets are on their way to destruction and want to take you with them. Turn from the false prophets. Turn back to the true prophet, who lives the truth, who is the truth. Jesus threw many analogies together in these paragraphs, but in them all He spoke the same thought: "Follow Me. Don't live as the world does."

The Two Claims to Heaven (Matt. 7:21–23)

The sermon's third concluding paragraph describes people who think they are following Jesus but are not. Perhaps a false prophet has deceived them; perhaps they have deceived themselves. In any case, Jesus does not recognize these people as His own. They have done great things for Jesus: They have proclaimed Jesus publicly; they have diligently fought evil and miraculously helped people in need—all in honor of Jesus. They sincerely desired to serve Jesus and did so in a most spectacular way. What's the problem? They chose to serve Jesus in a way they chose, rather than the way He chose for them. Jesus called people to obedience to the Father's plan (v. 21), not to spectacular self-chosen plans to serve the Father. Jesus, unfortunately, will send the latter group far from Him. They will be surprised when He announces their true character—**evildoers** (v. 23).

The Two Builders (Matt. 7:24–27)

Jesus wrapped up the sermon with one more series of contrasts, another way in which people can be deceived. Some supposed followers of Jesus praise themselves for the amount of time they spend listening to what Jesus has said. They read His words in the Bible;

they attend church where others sing and speak His words; they soak it all in. But Jesus points out the danger of stopping there. He does so by painting contrasting pictures of two types of people. But both types share one crucial common feature. Jesus noted that they both **hear these words of mine** (vv. 24, 26). But the similarity ends there. For only some hearers put Jesus' words **into practice**; others do not (vv. 24, 26). Jesus' analogy portrays their destinies graphically. The houses, the lives of those who only listen, fall into shreds. The houses, the lives of the obedient, stand firm.

Is Jesus here preaching of the possibility of earning salvation by what we do? Of course not. We need to compare these words with other statements Jesus made that call us to respond in faith to the grace He freely offers. Yet here He is making the crucial point that people who truly have been saved by grace will demonstrate their faith and God's grace by living lives of obedience.

WORDS FROM WESLEY

Not All Who Say, "Lord, Lord"

First, I am to consider the case of him who builds his house upon the sand. It is concerning him our Lord saith, "Not every one that saith unto me, Lord, Lord, shall enter into the kingdom of heaven." And this is a decree which cannot pass; which standeth fast for ever and ever. It therefore imports us, in the highest degree, throughly to understand the force of these words. Now what are we to understand by that expression, "That saith unto me, Lord, Lord?" It undoubtedly means, *that thinks of going to heaven by any other way than that which I have now described.* It therefore implies (to begin at the lowest point) all good words, all verbal religion. It includes whatever creeds we may rehearse, whatever professions of faith we make, whatever number of prayers we may repeat, whatever thanksgivings we read or say to God. . . . After I have thus successfully preached to others, still I myself may be a castaway. I may, in the hand of God, snatch many souls from hell, and yet drop into it when I have done. I may bring many others to the kingdom of heaven, and yet myself never enter there. Reader, if God hath ever blessed my word to *thy* soul, pray that He may be merciful to *me* a sinner! (WJW, vol. 5, 423)

DISCUSSION

Faith is not only a matter of our thoughts, but also of our actions.

1. What reasons might Jesus have had to talk about how hard it is to follow Him?

2. What might the rains and floods in this passage have represented to Jesus' original hearers? What do they represent in your life?

3. Do you think the metaphor comparing a wolf in sheep's clothing accurately describes false teachers? What similarities can you name?

4. A gate opens to a city or home. Where do the narrow and wide gates lead?

5. If Christians are the only example of Jesus that most people ever see, what would their perceptions of Christ be like by seeing your church? You?

6. If following Jesus is so difficult, why does anyone want to do it?

7. Why is it so easy to work the Bible into a lecture but so hard to work it into your life?

8. React to this statement: "Following Jesus is all or nothing; there is no maybe."

9. If your actions the past week were a headline, what would it read?

10. In what area of your life do you need to apply Christ's teachings more fully?

PRAYER

Father, may our actions and words align, and may both be pleasing to You. Amen.

6

THE COST OF DISCIPLESHIP

Matthew 10:32–42

To follow Jesus requires our total commitment.

Life is incredibly busy, and most people are forced to juggle many responsibilities. In the age in which we live, there are no clear lines between homemaker and accountant, dad and soccer coach, or church member and CEO. We all must manage many priorities each week, and all of them are important. Is it possible to have ten number-one priorities?

According to Jesus, the answer is no. Only one thing will have an ultimate claim on our attention, energy, and passion. We may choose family, career, success, health, or Christ as our first priority, but we cannot choose to honor them all equally.

This study will challenge you to examine your priorities and put Jesus Christ first in your life.

COMMENTARY

The context of this passage is Jesus calling and sending His disciples. Before looking at this context, we need to review. First, in the Sermon on the Mount, Jesus presented a theology of Christian faith and living. Rather than living as a sinful or selfish person, a Christian should live according to God's value system.

Second, Jesus performed a series of miracles. Many people received a "touch of the Master's hand" (Matt. 8:1—9:34). As a result of this ministry, three things became apparent: (1) There were many needy people; (2) Jesus had an important ministry to these people; and (3) more workers were needed.

The urgency of preaching the gospel of the kingdom and the magnitude of the needy people are the pressures under which Jesus selected and prepared His disciples for their work (9:35—10:42). He requested the disciples to pray for laborers. He then appointed the Twelve. He taught them how their needs would be supplied and how to minister, and warned them about the conflicts they would encounter.

In this passage, He talked to them about the depth of discipleship they would need. Not just the Twelve, but all who want to be His disciples need to check their attitudes, value systems, and priorities to see if we are effective servants of Jesus.

Jesus is calling His disciples to a commitment of devotion, a reevaluation of priorities, and a reconsideration of the cost of discipleship. It is true that a disciple cannot earn merit toward salvation. We are saved by grace, through faith (Eph. 2:8–9). It is also true that it is not always popular or easy to be a witness. Sometimes a disciple is the only one in his or her group who professes faith in Jesus. At times not only individuals but whole groups of Christians have been persecuted. God's people have paid huge prices for their faith.

This study calls for a confession of Christ, a supreme love for Christ that is worthy of Him, and a proper understanding of God's rewards.

Confessing Christ (Matt. 10:32–33)

In verses 32–33, Jesus offers His disciples two opposite conditional relationships. In simple terms, He is saying, "If you confess Me, then I will confess you. But if you deny Me, then I will deny you." The structure of the two opposite conditions does not permit one to choose one condition and expect the opposite response. If a person wants Jesus to confess him or her to God the Father, then he or she must fulfill the prerequisite condition to receive that reward. In today's churches many people have excused their failure of confessing Christ by saying that Jesus understands. He does. He understands denying Him reveals a broken relationship.

The Greek word for *confess* means to say the same thing. If a man named John is asked, "Is your name John?" the correct answer is "Yes, my name is John." Confession doesn't find ways to circumvent or evade the truth. When it comes to confession, Christ gives us two categories: confess or deny. The answer is either a confession or a denial of Him.

Sometimes it is difficult to confess Christ. In the verses preceding this passage, Jesus warned of opposition and persecution. Ever since the first generation of Christians, when Saul was leading the persecution, some have confessed Christ as martyrs. The word *martyr* is a transliteration of the phrase *to witness*. Christians have often witnessed for their faith in Christ in difficult situations, even as martyrs.

WORDS FROM WESLEY

Matthew 10:32–33

Thy confessor in deed and word,
Before the sons of men,
In all the tempers of my Lord
I would Thy cause maintain:
And if my Lord I thus confess,
Thou wilt Thy servant own,
Present before Thy Father's face,
And place me on Thy throne.
Ah, wretched souls, who urged by shame
Desert your Master's cause,
Before the world deny His name,
And stumble at His cross!
Disown'd before the heavenly host,
Ye shall receive your hire,
Out from His glorious presence thrust
Into eternal fire. (PW, vol. 10, 329)

If people fail to confess Christ, they have not only denied Him, but they have also denied their faith relationship with Him. Whether or not Jesus confesses us to His Father is intrinsically linked to our confession or lack thereof. This may seem hard, but a government expects its citizens to confess their homeland. A wife expects her husband to confess that he is married and intends to remain true to her. Christ expects Christians to do as much.

While Jesus stood trial before the high priest, Peter was accused of being one of His followers. Rather than confessing his allegiance, Peter denied even knowing Jesus. Later, Peter repented and Jesus restored him. Even though it can be difficult, Jesus calls His followers to confess Him.

Commitment Worthy of Christ (Matt. 10:34–39)

Since Christians have experienced God's love, they desire to share it with others. Since God's love has infused a genuine love in the Christian's own heart, he or she desires to give and receive *agape* love. The desire for peace is strong in Christians.

In the Jewish mind, the word *peace* often meant more than an end of fighting. If a person said "Peace" to another person, it also included a desire for all of God's blessing to be given to that person.

Jesus said He did not come to **bring peace** (v. 34). If the Prince of Peace did not come to bring peace, why did He come? He came to die, to atone for our sins. Jesus did not come so we could feel good with everyone, but to be our Savior.

Jesus came to bring the **sword** (v. 34). This sword was not a military weapon symbolizing power and splendor, but a long knife used for killing small animals and slicing meat, as a knife used in butchering. Even though Christians desire peace and love, this vivid picture predicts rejection, hostility, and persecution.

The strongest emotional bonds are those between parents and children. Yet Jesus said He came to **turn a man against his father, a daughter against her mother** (v. 35). He was saying that these strong ties may be painfully tested in regard to the kingdom of God when some family members accept Christ and others reject Him. In spite of our love, we may still feel the pain of the sword of conflict in our hearts.

Are we willing to place our love for Christ above human relationships?

WORDS FROM WESLEY
Matthew 10:34

For *Think not that I am come*—That is, think not that universal peace will be the immediate consequence of my coming. Just the contrary. Both public and private divisions will follow, wheresoever my Gospel comes with power. Yet this is not the design, though it be the event of his coming, through the opposition of devils and men. (ENNT)

Jesus is calling on His disciples to love Him **more than** (v. 37) they love their parents and children. He wants a love that surpasses the strongest love we possess. Anything less than first place puts Christ beneath the level of acceptable love. An inferior love for Jesus is not worthy of Him.

If we love anyone more than we love Jesus, then that person should be the object of our worship. Worship springs from the idea of "worthship," of being worthy of adoration. Worship is an act we render to the one we admire most. To love someone more than we love Jesus and then attempt to worship Jesus is incongruent and a conflict of ideas.

Are we willing to love Christ more than we love our own relationships and interests?

A disciple's love for Christ is to surpass everything, even life itself. **Anyone who does not take his cross and follow me is not worthy of me** (v. 38) calls the disciples to the superlative degree of love. Not only is our love to be the highest, but since Jesus spoke in the present tense, it is to be continually practiced. Daily, all of our Christian life, we are to take up our cross.

"Taking up our cross" is asking us, "For what are we willing to die?" Are we willing to lose our lives for Christ? Ironically, **whoever loses his life for** Christ **will find it** (v. 39). Those who seek to find their life apart from a faith commitment to Jesus Christ miss important elements of life.

Christ's Commissions (Matt. 10:40–42)

In the preceding verses, Jesus addressed His disciples. But in this section, He addresses those who will meet the disciples. Jesus is offering a series of rewards to those who accept His disciples and work to support them. These promises could be understood as blessings for those who help send missionaries and support their pastors by helping them in their ministry.

A reward is offered to those who receive His disciples. Not only that, but **he who receives you receives me, and he who receives me receives the one who sent me** (v. 40). Those who receive the gospel receive a relationship with God the Father. The first reward is saving faith. The second reward Jesus expresses is the **prophet's** and **righteous man's reward** (v. 41). Jesus said anyone who received a prophet or a righteous person would receive the same type of reward. So, what are those rewards?

Let's first look at the righteous person's reward. Do righteous people get paid for keeping the Ten Commandments, attending worship services, and doing noble things at home and in society? Of course not. The righteous person's reward is his or her personal relationship with God and the personal assurance that they have been true to their Lord and to themselves.

What is the reward of the prophet? The Bible answers this question in several different ways.

The prophet's remuneration is seldom mentioned in the Bible. Elijah was fed by the ravens, indicating that he was not paid during that terrible time of famine. Jeremiah, instead of being paid for his work, watched his book destroyed and then was placed in prison. From a financial and personal perspective, he would have been in better condition if he had not ministered. Some prophets, like Ezekiel, suffered the calamity of being taken prisoner of war along with others. They felt that their ministry was to a congregation of "dry bones." Their hearts were so broken that instead of singing praise to God, they hung up their harps and wept (Ps. 137).

The prophet's reward was greater than his pay. How much money is the book of Jeremiah worth? How much is the book of Isaiah worth? How valuable was the ministry of Elijah and Elisha? The value of a prophet is more than his or her pay. God's payday is not just on Friday. The greatest reward a prophet receives is the knowledge that he or she has fulfilled the calling of God, which money cannot buy.

In His third reward, Jesus is promising a blessing, even a payment, for giving aid to His servants. He is offering to bless one of the most common courtesies, giving a cup of cold water. Since Jesus takes note of such small act, shouldn't every Christian take the **cup of cold water** test (Matt. 10:42)? Just ask yourself, "Am I aiding or hindering the ministry of my church?"

God blesses those who pass the test. Among the common factors in healthy growing churches are a love for their pastor and the church ministries, and members' joyful help in ministry. Likewise, declining churches exhibit members' disharmony with their pastor and an unwillingness of members to participate in church ministry.

Jesus knew that not everyone would love Him supremely. Many would deny any relationship with Him. But Jesus called His disciples to help Him with His ministry. He challenged them to be committed to Him. He asked them to love Him more than they loved anyone else. Jesus was not only going to bless them, but also those who helped His disciples. And He asks the same of us today.

WORDS FROM WESLEY

Matthew 10:42

How small the gift it matters not
Given for the sake of Christ the Lord,
It cannot be by Christ forgot,
Or lose its infinite reward.
A cup of water shall procure
(Bestow'd for Jesus' sake alone)
Rivers of life, and raptures pure,
Which flow perennial from His throne. (PW, vol. 10, 244)

For those who receive the gospel, there is saving faith. Those who receive the ministry and support it will receive the same type of reward as the one doing it. Yes, even a cup of cold water in His name will be remembered.

DISCUSSION

When serving Christ is our priority, our faithfulness to Him will impact every decision we make.

1. What single word do you think best describes this teaching by Jesus?

2. What do you think the word *despise* means in this context?

3. In what ways did Jesus' life bring peace to earth? What divisions has it caused?

4. Why would Christ come between father and son or mother and daughter?

5. In practical terms, what do you think it means to forget self and become lost in God?

6. Jesus' message here lets followers know they are in for challenging times. In what ways do we present that message to new believers today?

7. React to this statement: "There is no such thing as cozy Christianity."

8. Based on this passage, what is the relationship between faith and action? How does this compare with other Bible passages you may know?

9. Jesus mentions a reward for those who receive Him. What do you think that reward is?

10. In what ways can we support one another in following Christ?

PRAYER

Father, we acknowledge our allegiance to Jesus Christ, Your Son. Help us take up our crosses and follow Him every day. Amen.

7

THE SABBATH GIFT

Matthew 11:28—12:14

The Sabbath is God's gift to us for refreshment of body and spirit.

It is ironic that we live in a culture where people are obsessed with leisure pursuits yet are over-busy, over-stressed, and have precious little time to enjoy life. We frequently bump up against the limits of our own time and energy, often making remarks such as "I wish I could clone myself," or "There just aren't enough hours in the day!"

God foresaw this problem, of course, and wisely provided a day of rest each week, a time to relax, refresh, and refocus our minds on what matters most. The fact that the Sabbath has been both abused and ignored does not alter God's perfect plan.

This study will challenge the mistaken assumption that we are too busy to relax.

COMMENTARY

Who was this man Jesus? See what authority He had! He spoke and a paralyzed man was healed and forgiven (Matt. 9:1–8), a dead girl came to life (9:18–26), the blind began to see and the dumb to speak (9:27–34). He sent out His disciples with this same power (10:1–42). These miracles were evidence that He was "the one who was to come" (11:3). Those who saw this evidence and yet rejected Him were worthy of judgment (11:20–24). Indeed, it was God who came in the person of Jesus. John the Baptist was the "Elijah" who prepared the people for Jesus' coming (11:14–15). As Jesus made His claims clearer, opposition became more pronounced.

Who are You, Jesus? See His answer in Matthew 11:25–30. Verses 25–27 provide necessary background for this study, which begins in verse 28. Jesus offers praise to the Father (vv. 25–26), tells us who He is (v. 27), and then offers rest to weary and burdened humankind (vv. 28–30). The incident that follows in 12:1–14 further clarifies who Jesus is and how we can receive this rest from Him.

Jesus praises the Father that, although He is "Lord of heaven and earth" (v. 25), He has not revealed himself to the "wise and learned" but to those who receive His revelation as "little children." This way of revealing himself is the Father's "good pleasure" (v. 26) because it shows His grace in making himself known to all. Human pride will never know the Father.

The Father has made himself known to the simple in no other way than through His Son—"all things have been committed to me by my Father" (v. 27). Since "no one knows the Father except the Son," only those to whom the Son reveals Him will know Him. To whom does the Son reveal Him? The wonderful answer to this question is found in verses 28–30.

I Will Give You Rest (Matt. 11:28–30)

Because the Father reveals himself only through the Son, Jesus can say, **Come to me** (v. 28). He invites **all you who are weary and burdened.** The proud may not admit their weariness. The haughty may laugh and say, "I have no burdens." But to all who will admit they are tired of trying to run their lives, Jesus says, **Come**. To all who are exhausted because they have been trying to prove themselves good enough by their own works, Jesus says, **Come**. Every person is in that invitation. *You* are included. The most immoral sinner is included. Only those who are too proud to come are excluded, because they exclude themselves.

And what will Jesus do when we come to Him? He **will give** us **rest** (v. 28). These are the very words of God found in Exodus 34:14.

Jesus will forgive; He will restore that relationship with God that brings deep rest to our souls. God himself will put within us a deep sense of our well-being in Him. Henceforth we will live life out of this rich relationship with the Father. When we come to Jesus, He invites us to **take** His **yoke upon** us (Matt. 11:29). This was an expression used by the Jews of Jesus' day for studying the law. The person who took the "yoke" of the law upon himself promised to study the law of Moses and live by it. But this is Jesus' yoke. It is the true understanding of the law that comes from Him. This is not a yoke of striving to be good by keeping rules, but a yoke of utter surrender to Christ. This surrender brings the deepest **rest for** our **souls**. God's peace penetrates to the very core of our beings.

WORDS FROM WESLEY

Matthew 11:28–29

28. *Come to me*—Here he shows to whom *he is pleased* to reveal these things; to the weary and heavy laden; *ye that labour*—After rest in God: *and are heavy laden*—With the guilt and power of sin: *and I will give you rest*—I alone (for none else can) *will* freely *give you* (what ye cannot purchase) *rest* from the guilt of sin by justification, and from the power of sin by sanctification.

29. *Take my yoke upon you*—Believe in me: receive me as your prophet, priest, and king. *For I am meek and lowly in heart*—Meek towards all men, lowly towards God: *and ye shall find rest*—Whoever therefore does not find rest of soul, is not meek and lowly. The fault is not in the yoke of Christ: but in thee, who hast not taken it upon thee. Nor is it possible for any one to be discontented, but through want of meekness or lowliness. (ENNT)

Although Jesus is one with the Father, He is **gentle** (v. 29) toward those who come to Him. He is **humble in heart**. Unlike the proud person who flaunts his or her morality, Jesus reaches down to the least of us—all the way from heaven. His **yoke is**

easy and His **burden is light** (v. 30) because He puts His own head in the yoke and carries the burden with us. We live now by His strength and His power. Who wouldn't want to bear His yoke? In the incidents recorded in Matthew 12:1–14, we find some people who didn't want Christ's yoke.

Lord of the Sabbath (Matt. 12:1–14)

These verses relate two incidents in which Jesus offended the Pharisees by what He did on the Sabbath. In verses 1–8, He allowed His hungry disciples to pick a few handfuls of grain and eat them. In verses 9–14, He healed a man with a shriveled hand. At the center of these two incidents is the key verse: **For the Son of Man is Lord of the Sabbath** (v. 8). Jesus is clearly claiming divine authority, because only God is Lord of the Sabbath. The purpose of the Sabbath is to honor Him, so He is the One with authority to tell us how it should be kept. The way He would have us keep it demonstrates the difference between Jesus' yoke and the legalistic yoke of the Pharisees.

The path of **Jesus** (v. 1) and His disciples passed through the **grainfields** on a certain **Sabbath**. By Jewish Law, any hungry person who passed by a field could pull off a few grains with his hand and eat. Jesus' disciples did not take scythes and begin to harvest the field. They merely reached out their hands to satisfy their hunger. The Pharisees' immediate response: **Your disciples are doing what is unlawful on the Sabbath** (v. 2). Your disciples are harvesting grain!

Jesus uses the Old Testament to show the fallacy of their statement. **Haven't you read** (v. 3) is a strong rebuke to people who were supposed to be educated in the Scriptures. A story from the life of David recorded in 1 Samuel 21:1–6, the law of Moses itself as found in Numbers 28:9, and the prophecy of Hosea 6:6, demonstrate the error of this legalistic approach to the Sabbath.

David (Matt. 12:3) and **his companions** did what Jesus' disciples were accused of doing; they broke the Mosaic law by eating—they **ate the consecrated bread** (v. 4) from the **house of God**. Only the priests were supposed to eat this bread. Why was David innocent? Because he and his men were in need, they **were hungry** (v. 3), running for their lives, and had no other source of food.

The disciples were accused of breaking the Sabbath. That is just what the **priests** do every Sabbath by working **in the temple** (v. 5)! Yet they are **innocent** because they do this work as part of their worship of God. The service of God takes precedence over a mere Sabbath regulation. And Jesus boldly announces **one greater than the temple is here** (v. 6). Jesus is the One greater than the temple, for He is the God who was worshiped in the temple. Thus He is the **Lord of the Sabbath** (v. 8) with authority to say how it should be kept.

WORDS FROM WESLEY

Matthew 12:8

Therefore they are guiltless, were it only on this account, that they act by my authority, and attend on me in my ministry, as the priests attended on God in the temple: *is Lord even of the Sabbath*— This certainly implies, that the Sabbath was an institution of great and distinguished importance; it may perhaps also refer to that signal act of authority which Christ afterward exerted over it, in changing it from the seventh to the first day of the week. (ENNT)

It is important to note that Jesus does not do away with the Sabbath. He does not abolish a weekly day when we rest from making a living and worship the living God. Jesus shows us how to keep this day in the right way. The words of God to the prophet Hosea are also the words of Jesus, the Lord of the Sabbath: **I desire mercy, not sacrifice** (v. 7; Hos. 6:6). Keep the Sabbath day out of reverence for God by showing compassion and concern for human need, not by the legalistic keeping of a set of rules.

How easy it is for us to manipulate a set of rules to our own ends! That is just what these Pharisees had been doing. Many Jewish teachers of their day would not have objected to what the disciples did in the grain field. Was taking a few heads of grain and eating them really "working" on the Sabbath? These Pharisees used their rule as occasion to accuse Jesus. How often we use our rules as an excuse to do what we want to do. We have so reacted to the Pharisees that we have made a new rule: "It's OK to do almost anything on the Lord's Day." Do we keep the Lord's Day in devotion to God or for the amusement of ourselves? Are we showing compassion when, for our own convenience, we rob other people of their Sabbath rest by shopping in stores and eating in restaurants on the Lord's Day?

Jesus is no longer out on the pathway passing a field. He has entered **their synagogue** (Matt. 12:9), the Jewish place of worship. In the synagogue, of all places, one must keep the Sabbath properly! Jesus' enemies thought that the **man with a shriveled hand** (v. 10) would be a good occasion to trap Jesus into violating the Sabbath. Certainly Jesus would **heal on the Sabbath**. They would be able to **accuse** Him of law breaking. Jesus, however, uses this occasion to show us how we should keep the Sabbath in a way that pleases the God of the Sabbath.

Jewish teachers often argued from the lesser case to the greater. Jesus follows this line of argument. His hearers agreed that if **a sheep . . . falls into a pit on the Sabbath**, it was quite right to **take hold of it and lift it out** (v. 11). Who can deny that a human being is **much more valuable . . . than a sheep** (v. 12)? Therefore it must be right to do an act of mercy and heal the man with the withered hand on the Sabbath. The Sabbath was a celebration of God's deliverance from bondage. Jesus' miracles were God's deliverance in action. How absurd to think that He could not deliver on the day that celebrated deliverance. **Therefore it is lawful to do good on the Sabbath** (v. 12). In fact, there is no day more appropriate for doing good to others. There are two sides to the coin of Sabbath observance: honor God by resting from what we do to make a living and show love and compassion to others.

Jesus demonstrates what He has said by healing the man, whose hand **was completely restored, just as sound as the other** (v. 13). The Pharisees were not able to establish a clear legal case against Jesus. His argument from the lesser case of a sheep to the greater case of a human being was cogent. But they rejected His authority to give the true meaning of the Sabbath. They rejected His claim to be Lord of the Sabbath. Rather than applauding the liberating work of God in restoring the man's hand, the Pharisees immediately began to plan **how they might kill Jesus** (v. 14).

WORDS FROM WESLEY

Matthew 12:13

The word of Christ alone
New life and vigour gives
Who first our helplessness makes known,
And then our souls relieves:
Like wither'd hands they are,
Yet strength if He ordain,
We stretch them forth to God by prayer,
By alms and helps to man. (PW, vol. 10, 258)

Jesus calls us to recognize Him as Lord of the Sabbath and Lord of our lives. He calls us to keep the Lord's Day by devoting the day to God and showing mercy to others. This keeping of the Sabbath is a celebration of the rest Jesus gives us when we take on His yoke. Coming to Jesus is not a matter of keeping a list of rules. It is a matter of unreserved devotion to Him expressed in mercy and compassion for others.

DISCUSSION

When we practice Sabbath rest, we learn restraint and practice trust in God.

1. Describe the conflict within this story. Who is at odds? Why? What is the result?

2. In what ways did the strict Sabbath observers get it wrong? Did they get anything right?

3. When Jesus uses the word *rest*, what do you think He means?

4. What does it mean to keep a Sabbath day holy?

5. Why do you think God created the Sabbath?

6. Do you agree with this statement: "We rest not to be healthy but because God said so"? Explain.

7. How do you balance doing good things for others and taking time out for yourself?

8. Why do you think the Sabbath is not observed as seriously among Christians today?

9. What are some practical ways of honoring the Sabbath without becoming legalistic?

10. When you give God your time, what will He give back?

PRAYER

Lord of the Sabbath, remind us of our need of rest. Help us to follow Your example. Amen.

EYES TO SEE THE TRUTH

Matthew 13:1–23

The ability to understand biblical principles is directly related
to the attitude of one's heart.

How can one person hear the good news about Jesus and
respond positively, while another can listen to the same message
and remain unchanged? That question has troubled Christians
for a long time. It has obvious implications for evangelism and
may also cause us to doubt the veracity of what we believe. Is
the gospel true for us but not true for everyone? While truth is
objective, our experience of it is highly subjective. Our ability
to perceive spiritual truths depends on our spiritual openness.

This study explores some of the reasons some people may
accept Christ while others reject Him. You will be challenged to
examine your own level of spiritual receptivity and to become
more sensitive to the spiritual condition of those around you.

COMMENTARY

Matthew's gospel is a gospel of the kingdom. The author takes
the reader through the announcement of the kingdom (ch. 4),
when Jesus comes on the scene after John is imprisoned. The
message of Jesus is similar to John's and is just as simple:
"Repent, for the kingdom of heaven is near." Next, Matthew
records Jesus teaching the principles of kingdom living (ch. 5–7).
The Sermon on the Mount shows how the kingdom should look
in the lives of those who are disciples of Jesus. We are to be poor
in spirit, pure in heart, meek, and believers who live out the law
in the way we love each other and those who hate and use us. It

is in chapter 13 that we are given practical examples of what the kingdom is like, through Jesus' use of parables.

The concept of the kingdom of God is wrapped up in a personal, life-transforming relationship with God. It would be a mistake to try to make it something less personal than that. The kingdom evolves and emerges in the hearts and lives of believers as they allow God to rule and reign in their lives. Discipleship, then, is living out the kingdom on a daily basis. The teachings of Jesus in the Sermon on the Mount instruct the disciples how to live life as citizens of the kingdom; the parables of the kingdom demonstrate how God works the kingdom out in us. The parable of the sower is about the way in which our hearts respond to "the sower."

In the gospel of Matthew, this parable is preceded by Jesus' statement about the Lord of the harvest (9:37–38). In chapters 11 and 12, John doubts Jesus is the Messiah (11:1–3), and Jesus pronounces woe on the unrepentant cities of the region (11:20–24). He is criticized by the religious leaders (12:1–14), accused by the Pharisees of working through the Devil (12:24), and challenged to show a sign of His authority and power (12:38). It is no wonder Jesus teaches in chapter 13 about hearing and understanding the message of the kingdom. He was speaking against a people who, like a child, stick their fingers in their ears and say, "I can't hear you." His heart was set on a harvest; theirs were hardened.

The Kingdom Demonstrated (Matt. 13:1–9)

Much of the ministry and teaching of Jesus occurred by the sea. This time, the sea was advantageous, acting as a natural reflector for the voice of Jesus as He spoke to the waiting crowd of people on the shore. The picture of the crowd standing and Jesus sitting is typical of the teaching posture of the day. In this manner, He began to teach them **many things in parables** (v. 3). The word *parable* literally means to put alongside of, or, in other words, to make a comparison. Parables were the usual teaching tool of Jewish rabbis. The simple people of Palestine liked examples taken from their everyday lives.

WORDS FROM WESLEY

Matthew 13:3

In parables—The word is here taken in its proper sense, for apt similes or comparisons. This way of speaking, extremely common in the eastern countries, drew and fixed the attention of many, and occasioned the truths delivered to sink the deeper into humble and serious hearers. At the same time, by an awful mixture of justice and mercy, it hid them from the proud and careless. (ENNT)

In this case, Jesus used a very familiar picture of sowing a field. Most all of the people gathered on the shore that day would have been familiar with the process of planting crops. In Jesus' day, the farmer would take a bag of seed and scatter it by hand over a given area. He would immediately plow the ground, thus covering the seed. In this manner, some seed would be lost to the unplowed ground and others to the thorns and rocks. However, the farmer was expecting a harvest from the seed that fell into the fertile ground.

Notice that Jesus doesn't focus on the farmer. His focus isn't even on the seed. His focus is on the soil. The seed is cast on all soil, regardless of the outcome. Some soil was considered **the path** (v. 4). It was out of reach of the plow and so the **birds came and ate** the seed that fell there. Some soil was **rocky** (v. 5). The shallow dirt was heated by the layer of rock below the surface. Because of the heat, the seed germinated faster, and the plant **sprang up quickly**. But, because the **soil was shallow** and the roots could not go deep, the plant was unable to draw nourishment and water from the depths of the soil. The **plants were**

scorched (v. 6) as soon as the sun came out. Still, some soil shared its space with **thorns** (v. 7). These thorns **choked the plants** and they died. However, some seed **fell on good soil** (v. 8). This soil was plowed, fertile, and therefore produced quite a crop, **a hundred, sixty or thirty times what was sown**. The seed was good in all cases; the soil was the deciding factor. **He who has ears, let him hear** (v. 9). The Hebrew concept of hearing has more to do with obedience to what was heard than auditory effectiveness. Jesus was effectively saying, "If you are ready to actively seek to do God's will and be a part of His kingdom, hear and obey what I am saying about your hearts."

WORDS FROM WESLEY
Matthew 13:4–7

And while he sowed, some seeds *fell by the highway-side, and the birds came and devoured them*—It is observable, that our Lord points out the grand hinderances of our bearing fruit, in the same order as they occur. The first danger is, that the birds will devour the seed. If it escape this, there is then another danger, namely, lest it be scorched, and wither away. It is long after this that the thorns spring up and choke the good seed.

A vast majority of those who hear the word of God, receive the seed as by the *highway-side*. Of those who do not lose it by the birds, yet many receive it as *on stony places*. Many of them who receive it in a better soil, yet suffer *the thorns to grow up, and choke it:* so that few even of these endure to the end, and bear fruit unto perfection: yet in all these cases, it is not the will of God that hinders, but their own voluntary perverseness. (ENNT)

The Method Defended (Matt. 13:10–17)

There is something natural about students questioning the method of their teachers. The disciples, upon hearing Jesus teach the people with this parable, began to question His method, saying, **Why do you speak to the people in parables?** (v. 10). The fact is, many people don't want to hear what God is saying about their hearts. The **secrets of the kingdom** (v. 11) are for the ones who are receptive to God's work and to His Word, not to those who are self-righteous and self-sufficient. **Whoever has** (v. 12) refers to the ones who are ready and willing to hear, and to them the reward is given. The Jews had been given much by God, including His Son. But those who are not willing to hear, **even what** they have **will be taken from** them.

WORDS FROM WESLEY

Matthew 13:12–13

12. *Whosoever hath*—That is, improves what he hath, uses the grace given according to the design of the giver; *to him shall be given*—More and more, in proportion to that improvement. *But whosoever hath not*—Improves it not, *from him shall be taken even what he hath*. Here is the grand rule of God's dealing with the children of men: a rule fixed as the pillars of heaven. This is the key to all His providential dispensations; as will appear to men and angels in that day.

13. *Therefore I speak to them in parables, because seeing, they see not*—In pursuance of this general rule, I do not give more knowledge to this people, because they use not that which they have already: having all the means of seeing, hearing, and understanding, they use none of them: they do not effectually see, or hear, or understand any thing. (ENNT)

Jesus identified the Jews as the fulfillment of Isaiah's prophecy, **ever hearing but never understanding . . . ever seeing but never perceiving** (v. 14). Their hardened hearts kept them from hearing Jesus' words. Often people understand Jesus' words here to say that He did not want the Jews to hear. **Otherwise they might see** (v. 15) does not indicate God's unwillingness for the Jews to see, but rather indicates what they say about themselves: "We don't want to hear You, otherwise we would have to turn from our ways." Notice instead God's willingness to **heal them**. It is with great sadness that Jesus quoted Isaiah 6:9. It is not that the parables are to make the message harder to understand; in fact, the message is simpler. The Jewish leaders held to an "ignorance is bliss" position when it came to the message of God. Jesus was making it as simple as possible for those who wanted to hear what God said to them. The religious leaders stumbled over the simplicity. And yet, the disciples were **blessed** (v. 16) because they could **see** (this implies genuine experience, and not mere intellectual understanding) and **hear** (indicating obedience).

The Parable Defined (Matt. 13:18–23)

In the final section of this text, Jesus gave the disciples a private lesson in the meaning of the parable. The four types of soils listed in the parable indicate four types of **heart** (v. 19), or four ways in which we respond to the Word. God is trying to make us into something. He is making us into fruitful plants, and He sows the seed for a harvest.

The first soil is the hardened heart. This is the heart that **hears the message about the kingdom** (v. 19), and yet does not **understand it**. The word *understand* does not only mean that the person is unable to intellectually understand it, but that he or she is not grasping it. It is not so much an inability as a lack of desire. The heart of the hearer has to be prepared for the Word. To be fertile, one must be broken up and prepared to hear what God has to say. If the heart is not ready, the Word cannot sink in. That heart is much like a **path**, hard and trodden down. Seeds do not germinate there, they only hit the surface. In fact, the seed does not stay on the surface long because the **evil one** comes and **snatches away** the seed through distraction and deceit. In that way, the seed sown has no effect on the hearer.

The second soil is the shallow heart. These are the hearers who, when the Word is sown in their hearts, **receive it with joy**

(v. 20). The enthusiasm of their hearts is to be commended, but it is not enough. The joy lasts for only a short time, because they are too shallow. Matthew uses the word *proskairos*, or temporary. Just as the rock allows for quick germination, this one probably doesn't really think through what is heard; he or she is only interested in the thrill, so he or she reacts quickly. However, because **he** or she **has no root** (v. 21), his or her faith doesn't last. This time, it isn't the Devil that comes to snatch it away, but **trouble or persecution**. While joy and excitement are great to see in a believer, faith cannot be based on these alone. The believer must be grounded in more than feelings. An intimate relationship with the Source of life must be maintained. The Word must become a part of who we are. Faith must be the lifeline to growth. Without these things, there can be no root. Be assured, the sun is coming out. The heat is going to beat down on believers. Whether or not believers can draw nourishment to withstand is based on whether or not they have put down roots.

WORDS FROM WESLEY

Matthew 13:22

He that received the seed among the thorns, is he that heareth the word and considereth it—in spite of Satan and his agents: Yea, *hath root in himself*, is deeply convinced, and in a great measure inwardly changed; so that he will not draw back, even *when tribulation or persecution ariseth*. And yet even in him, together with the good seed, *the thorns spring up* [ver. 7] (perhaps unperceived at first) till they gradually *choke* it, destroy all its life and power, *and it becometh unfruitful*.

Cares are *thorns* to the poor: wealth to the rich; the desire of other things to all. *The deceitfulness of riches*—Deceitful indeed! for they smile, and betray: kiss, and smite into hell. They put out the eyes, harden the heart, steal away all the life of God; fill the soul with pride, anger, love of the world; make men enemies to the whole cross of Christ! And all the while are eagerly desired, and vehemently pursued, even by those who believe there is a God! (ENNT)

The third soil is the divided heart This is good ground. Yet, the intrusion of other things keeps these hearts from bearing fruit. **The worries of this life and the deceitfulness of wealth** (v. 22) creep into the life of the believers and pull them between their faith and their "things." It is impossible to be fruitful while caught in the trap of these cruel thorns and pulled between two masters (6:24).

What then is good soil? Good soil is prepared and fertile. The fourth soil is the receptive heart. The true believer **hears the word** (13:23) like the others. True believers' hearts, however, are prepared to **understand** the Word. They grasp it and apply it to their lives. They allow the roots to go deep into who they are, and they draw their nourishment and strength from their faith. In them, the sower finds a **crop** producing fruit in various amounts. Some produce a **hundred**, some **sixty or thirty times what was sown.** Jesus offered no criticism for the varied amounts, understanding that not all believers produce at the same rate. God is interested in producing fruit-bearing disciples. He gives us everything needed to be productive. However, He allows us to participate in His harvest as the soil.

DISCUSSION

If the seed of God's Word is to grow, we must nurture the soil in which it is planted.

1. What is represented by the various elements of this story— seed, soil types, thorns, crop, and so forth?

2. Jesus quoted Isaiah 6:9–10. Refer to that passage. What similarities do you note between the call of Isaiah and the ministry of Jesus?

3. Name some reasons why people might fail to perceive the truth that seems so obvious to you.

4. What things might we do to help open their eyes to see the truth more clearly?

5. List some factors that might hinder a person from growing in the faith after accepting Christ.

6. In what ways might we support people who have made a decision to follow Jesus?

7. Do you think unbelievers are the only ones with "rocky soil," or could this also apply to someone who is already a Christian? Why or why not?

8. This passage describes Christians as seed sowers. Are we also required to be seed nurturers and seed harvesters? Why or why not?

9. Describe a time when you knew you were supposed to speak to someone, though it seemed the person might not be receptive.

10. Share your conversion experience.

PRAYER

Heavenly Father, help us to be plowed, worked, and watered that we might be good fields for Your harvest. Amen.

9

JUSTICE DELAYED

Matthew 13:24–30, 36–43

Jesus will return to judge the wicked and reward the righteous.

If God is good, why do the wicked seem to prosper? That question was famously asked by Jeremiah (Jer. 12:1) but has also been voiced by Job (Job 21:7), the psalmist (Ps. 73:16), and just about anyone who has ever suffered while trying to do what is right. Life just doesn't seem fair sometimes.

What we often forget is that the kingdom of heaven is like a football game in that the only score that matters is the one at the very end. While life may seem unfair, there will be a judgment that rights the scales permanently, and Jesus Christ will be the Judge!

This study will help you take the long view on justice in the church, the world, and in your own life.

COMMENTARY

For centuries the Jews had been awaiting a messiah, a political liberator who would inaugurate the kingdom of God on earth. But Jesus came preaching a different message concerning the kingdom, one the Jews had great difficulty comprehending because of their preconceived ideas. In the book of Matthew, there are fifty references to the kingdom; it was Jesus' primary teaching. Here in chapter 13, Jesus shares seven parables to help His disciples discern the true nature of the kingdom of heaven. The kingdom was more than just a future hope; it was also a present reality. The kingdom was not earthly and temporal; it was spiritual and eternal.

Four of the parables Jesus taught in Matthew 13 are found only here: the parable of the weeds, the parables of the hidden treasure and the pearl of great price, and the parable of the net. Each of the parables in chapter 13, with the exception of the parable of the sower, begins with, "The kingdom of heaven is like . . ." The form Jesus used here is much like that of the rabbinic teachers of His day. "The phrase meant that the subject was being explained by the whole analogy that followed, not just by the next word" (*Bible Background Commentary*). We must be careful not to equate the kingdom with the mustard seed, yeast, or "a man who sowed good seed" (v. 24). Instead, the totality of the parable highlights a principle to help us better understand the kingdom. We also must avoid the temptation to take the analogy further than intended or to attempt to allegorize every aspect of the story. It is precisely because no one object or illustration can fully explain the kingdom that Jesus offered seven distinct parables at this point.

WORDS FROM WESLEY

Matthew 13:24

He proposed another parable—in which He farther explains the case of unfruitful hearers. *The kingdom of heaven* (as has been observed before) sometimes signifies eternal glory: sometimes the way to it, inward religion; sometimes, as here, the Gospel dispensation: the phrase is likewise used for a person or thing relating to any one of those: so in this place it means, Christ preaching the Gospel, who *is like a man sowing good seed*—The expression, *is like*, both here and in several other places, only means, That the thing spoken of may be illustrated by the following similitude. *Who sowed good seed in his field*—God sowed nothing but good in His whole creation. Christ sowed only the good seed of truth in His church. (ENNT)

As we approach verse 24, Jesus just finished the parable of the sower, revealing to His disciples the varied responses to the message of the gospel. The Jews mistakenly believed that the Messiah would turn Israel and all nations to himself, but Jesus taught through this parable that individuals must respond to the message of the kingdom. Now Jesus turned His attention to another misunderstanding: The Jews believed the Messiah and Israel would one day rule over the entire world. In verses 24–30, Jesus informed them that the kingdom exists now in the midst of the world, and the final separation of good and evil will not occur until the end of the age.

The Reality of the Kingdom and the Origin of Evil in the World (Matt. 13:24–28, 36–39)

The content of the parable is quite simple: **a man . . . sowed good seed in his field.**

WORDS FROM WESLEY
Matthew 13:37

Yes we joyfully confess,
Thou the Son of God and man
Giv'st the principle of grace,
Sow'st in all that heavenly grain,
Saints through Thy engrafted word
Rise, the planting of the Lord.
Till the grain becomes a tree
Striking deep the root below
Through Thy Spirit's energy,
Imperceptibly they grow;
Late to full perfection rise,
Sinking, till they reach the skies. (PW, vol. 10, 275)

But while everyone was sleeping, his enemy came and sowed weeds among the wheat (v. 25). In verses 37–39, Jesus explained the parable to His questioning disciples: **The one who sowed the good seed is the Son of Man. The field is the world,**

and the good seed stands for the sons of the kingdom. The weeds are the sons of the evil one, and the enemy who sows them is the devil.

It should be noted that the seed in this parable, whether good or bad, refers to people, not to the Word of God or the message of the previous parable.

WORDS FROM WESLEY

Matthew 13:37

So at ten I began reading Prayers to such a congregation as I apprehend hardly ever assembled in this church before. I preached on Luke 8:18, part of the second lesson. Not a breath was heard; all was still "as summer's noontide air;" and I believe our Lord then sowed seed in many hearts, which will bring forth fruit to perfection.

After dinner I preached at Westwood-side. The high wind was a little troublesome; but the people regarded it not. We concluded the day with one of the most solemn love-feasts I have known for many years. (JJW, vol 4. 187)

Many scholars have tried to interpret this parable as an illustration of the church today—that good and bad grow side by side, only to be separated at the end of time. But Jesus specifically tells us the field is the world, not the kingdom. He was explaining to His disciples the origin of evil in the world—it is not from God, but from the Enemy, the Devil. Satan himself is the one who sowed weeds among the wheat. Evil people are the result of a deliberate cultivation by the Enemy. The fact that he did this while everyone was sleeping does not mean that God wasn't watching, since we know He never sleeps (Ps. 121:3–4). The phrase merely reveals to us that the Devil is sneaky and deceptive.

Most commentators believe the weed mentioned here is darnel, which in its early stages looks much like wheat. Only when the ears appear can it be recognized for what it truly is. Under normal circumstances, fields were weeded in the spring, but the weeds in this parable must have been discovered too late to have been pulled without harming the wheat; their roots may have already become intertwined.

Theologian Adam Clarke takes a different view. Noting the similarity between the Greek word used here for weeds ("tares" in KJV) and various Hebrew and Chaldean words, Clarke concludes that these "weeds" are "degenerate wheat," wheat that is far inferior, with smaller heads and a less productive crop. His conclusion is interesting, since the calamity of the fall in Genesis 3 is that humankind became degenerate because of the deception of the serpent. People did not become a separate species (like weeds among wheat), but they became degenerate, unproductive, and evil to the core.

WORDS FROM WESLEY
Matthew 13:28

He said, An enemy hath done this—A plain answer to the great question concerning the origin of evil. God made men (as He did angels) intelligent creatures, and consequently free either to choose good or evil: but He implanted no evil in the human soul: *An enemy* (with man's concurrence) *hath done this*.

Darnel, in the church, is properly outside Christians, such as have the form of godliness, without the power. Open sinners, such as have neither the form nor the power, are not so properly darnel, as thistles and brambles: these ought to be rooted up without delay, and not suffered in the Christian community.—Whereas should fallible men attempt to *gather up the darnel*, they would often *root up the wheat with them.* (ENNT)

Jesus' initial phrase, **The kingdom of heaven is like** (Matt. 13:24), is not in the present tense as it is translated. Instead, Jesus used the aorist passive, meaning "the kingdom of heaven has become like . . ." In the garden of Eden, God's kingdom was firmly established. He ruled in the hearts of people and so His kingdom was in effect on earth. But Satan sowed weeds, and so the "kingdom of heaven has become like" what we see illustrated in this parable. Now, because of the fall, God's kingdom exists amid evil, and so it will not be established in its fullness until that evil is gone.

The Reason for Delay (Matt. 13:28–30)

The servants asked him, "Do you want us to go and pull them up?" (v. 28). Jesus never explained to His disciples who these servants were. Perhaps they were angels. Or perhaps they had no correlation to reality, but merely expressed what the disciples were thinking: "Why don't we just get rid of the evil people now so God's kingdom will come?" After all, hadn't God commanded the Israelites when they entered the Promised Land to kill all the evil inhabitants? Surely, if God's kingdom has come, the evil ones should be removed. Such is human logic.

The one who sowed the good seed responded, **No . . . because while you are pulling the weeds, you may root up the wheat with them. Let both grow together until the harvest** (vv. 29–30). Is Jesus saying we should peacefully coexist with evil people and simply wait patiently for the harvest? Should we tolerate evil and hatred in the world? Or is He looking at the situation from a different angle?

Paul made it clear that we are to "expel the wicked man from among you" (1 Cor. 5:13), meaning we should not tolerate those who claim to be Christians but are not living as children of God. Evil should be expelled immediately from the church. But, remember, Jesus is not giving a parable about the church, but about the world. In the same passage Paul said, "What business is it of mine to judge those outside the church? . . . God will judge those outside" (5:12–13). From a human standpoint, it is often difficult to tell the difference between wheat and weeds. Sometimes we're misled by a weed's philanthropy and apparent "goodness" and think it surely must be wheat. At other times we misjudge wheat and declare it to be nothing but weeds. But it is God who looks at the heart. For us to prejudge and predetermine who is a weed and who is wheat before we see the fruit could be disastrous. Jesus told His disciples, "By their fruit you will recognize them" (Matt. 7:16), but we don't always see the fruit until the end. Only God knows which is a weed and which is wheat even before the harvest. We are not to judge (condemn); we leave ultimate judgment to God.

Perhaps a better way to look at this passage is in light of Jesus' previous teachings in Matthew: We are to be the "light of the world" (5:14) and "the salt of the earth" (5:13). By coexisting with the weeds, could it be possible that they might be converted to wheat? This would be possible if we take Adam Clarke's interpretation of the weeds as degenerate wheat—wheat that could subsequently be regenerated. Jesus may be explaining why there is a delay in judgment, why the servants should wait until the final harvest: Some of the wheat (or degenerate wheat that has the opportunity to become wheat and just may do so) may be uprooted (see 2 Pet. 3:9).

The Result of Final Judgment (Matt. 13:30, 39–43)

Jesus wanted to assure His disciples that the day is coming when the wheat and tares will certainly be divided: the harvest.

In a field, darnel, if not weeded out in the spring, must be left to grow until the harvest. Once the ears open, however, it becomes obvious which is the weed and which is the wheat. The farmer could then easily discard the weeds and harvest the wheat. And so it will be at **the end of the age** (v. 39).

The harvest is often associated in Scripture with God's judgment (Jer. 51:33; Joel 3:12–13; Rev. 14:14–19). For the farmer, the harvest is the final culmination of all his labors. It is the end. And so Jesus describes the harvest as the end of the age.

The Son of Man will send out his angels, and they will weed out of his kingdom everything that causes sin and all who do

evil (Matt. 13:41). Here it would appear that **kingdom** is equivalent to the field, but most commentators agree that, since the entire universe belongs to God, the world could properly be called His kingdom. There is no indication that Jesus was equating the kingdom with the church. Notice that the totality of sin and evil will be done away with—along with every person who committed evil. Their fate is certain: **They will** be thrown **into the fiery furnace, where there will be weeping and gnashing of teeth** (v. 42). The image here is one of fire and the ultimate judgment of God. **Weeping and gnashing of teeth** is used six times by Matthew and once by Luke, but nowhere else in the New Testament. **Weeping** suggests sorrow and grief, and **gnashing of teeth** refers to physical pain and torment (resulting in grinding the teeth, *Bible Knowledge Commentary*). The judgment is both painful and final.

In contrast, **the righteous will shine like the sun in the kingdom of their Father** (v. 43). This same description is given by Daniel concerning the fate of the righteous at the end of time (Dan. 12:3). But just as the kingdom is both a future hope and a present reality, so our shining may be both future and present: We are to be "without fault in a crooked and depraved generation, in which [we] shine like the stars in the universe as [we] hold out the word of life" (Phil. 2:15–16).

For the Jewish people who thought they had the kingdom figured out, Jesus revealed that their perceptions were all wrong. The kingdom was a present reality, even though evil had not yet been obliterated. There would be a delay in that part of His plan. But they could be assured that such a day would come. He spoke in parables, but He offered, **He who has ears, let him hear** (Matt. 13:43). They heard physically, but Jesus was inviting them to perceive, to understand. We, too, must read the Scriptures with our ears open—not just to hear, but to understand. We must often toss out our preconceived ideas and allow Scripture to teach us anew and afresh.

DISCUSSION

While we often desire justice for others, we prefer mercy for ourselves.

1. What is represented by the various items in these verses — field, wheat, weeds, enemy, harvest?

2. Why was the timing of the removal of weeds so important?

3. In what ways do the wheat and weeds grow together in your community?

4. Is Jesus saying we should tolerate sin in the church? Explain.

5. Do you think it is possible to distinguish a genuine believer from a hypocrite? Why do you think as you do?

6. Who is responsible for judging evil in the world?

7. What might happen if a person took on the job of weed puller without permission?

8. What is the best way to respond when you see evil in the world?

9. What can you do to guard your heart against any "weeds" that might spring up?

PRAYER

O Lord, we long for Your harvest that will separate the wheat from the weeds. But until that day, keep us growing faithfully in You. Amen.

10

PARABLES OF THE KINGDOM

Matthew 13:31–35, 44–50

Though it starts small, the kingdom of heaven will
grow into a powerful force.

Anyone familiar with the Old Testament knows that God
delights in producing great results from small beginnings.
David, the young man who killed the giant, and Gideon, the
unlikely hero who routed a vast army, are prime examples. In
spite of this, our attention is easily captured by that which is
flashy, spectacular, or grand in appearance. Forgetting that Jesus
began His mission with only a few disciples, we may question
whether or not our work is effective when compared to the
wealth, power, and prestige we see in business, government, or
other pursuits.

This study will give you both greater patience and greater
confidence as you wait for God to work in your life and in your
world.

COMMENTARY

For us to adequately understand the meanings of the parables
in these two passages, we will need to be sensitive to the fact
that each one teaches one—and only one—aspect of the kingdom.
We must not read into any parable more than is being taught by
our Lord. On the other hand, we must not remain on the surface
in our thinking; to understand the parables, we must look at their
cultural context, harmonize the interpretation with the other
parables, and follow good grammatical rules in developing the
interpretation.

Jesus was teaching in a primarily rural, farming society; thus, the parables concerning sowing and a tiny mustard seed. He was teaching women who knew how to handle kitchen duties; thus, the parable concerning yeast. The Master was teaching businessmen who knew the value of finding treasure and seeking fine pearls. He was teaching disciples who had left the life of the fisherman and were knowledgeable of the special nets used in that trade.

The Master Teacher always used the visual imagery with which His audience was familiar, and He never had to stretch for spiritual insights to come from His parables—they always adequately and obviously illustrated the truth He desired to bring to understanding.

WORDS FROM WESLEY

Matthew 13:31–32

31. *He proposed to them another parable*—The former parables relate chiefly to unfruitful hearers; these that follow, to those who bear good fruit. *The kingdom of heaven*—Both the Gospel dispensation, and the inward kingdom.

32. *The least*—That is, one of the least: a way of speaking extremely common among the Jews. *It becometh a tree*—In those countries it grows exceeding large and high. So will the Christian doctrine spread in the world, and the life of Christ in the soul. (ENNT)

Small Inception (Matt. 13:31–32)

Jesus said, **The kingdom of heaven is like a mustard seed** (v. 31). He tells us that the mustard seed is **the smallest of all your seeds** (v. 32). Actually, the cedar seed is the smallest of the seeds of that area, but the smallest one with which the people listening that day would be familiar was the mustard seed. They would have grown mustard as an herb and recognized how it started small and grew into **the largest of garden plants and becomes a tree**. The end result is that **birds of the air come and perch in its branches.**

Many movements have begun with a small group or even just one person. The Reformation began with just one Martin Luther, whom God used to challenge the liturgical systems of his day. The great revivals of history have begun with just a John Wesley, John Calvin, Charles Finney, Dwight Moody, and so on. In the truest sense, Jesus Christ was the beginning of the kingdom of heaven on this earth. By the time of the ascension, His band had grown to at least one hundred twenty, who were gathering in the upper room until the day of Pentecost. From that place and event, the church of Jesus Christ spread across the world in every direction and will continue to do so until the day when those from every nation will be gathered around the throne of God to crown their Founder as King of Kings and Lord of Lords.

At times every Christian worker questions if he or she is getting anything done for the sake of eternity. Every congregation wonders from time to time if they are just spinning their wheels instead of making real progress for the cause of Jesus Christ. Take heart. The church is fulfilling the purpose of Christ when it provides a refuge for souls of all nations, ethnic backgrounds, and walks of life. As long as the church is a haven of safety for all who would seek shelter from the storms of life, it is doing the will of the Founder.

Subtle Influence (Matt. 13:33)

We must shift our focus from the garden now to the kitchen. The woman of the house is preparing to bake bread. In that preparation she takes a small lump of dough left over from the last bread baking, today called "starter." This small lump she works **all through the dough** until it is no longer distinguishable; however, the effect is quite visible—the bread rises.

At times the church operates openly and quite vocally; other times it is driven underground and its voice becomes silent. In both times, the church maintains its influence throughout society. The church did not openly champion the cause for women's rights, but no movement in all the earth has done more for the status of women than the gospel of Jesus Christ. The church did not loudly protest in the face of many social ills, but the great revivals of history have done more to spare nations serious revolt than any other force. Wherever the church exists, its influence is realized, because its people permeate the society. People do not always see its presence, but they do see the influence of its presence. Like the small lump of starter, the church works its way into all levels of the social system and, whether openly or subtly, makes its presence known.

WORDS FROM WESLEY

The Need to Be Leaven in the Church

Our Church teaches, in the twenty-eighth Article, that "the unworthiness of the Minister does not hinder the validity of the sacraments." Although, therefore, there are many disagreeable circumstances, yet I advise all our friends to keep to the Church. God has surely raised us up for the Church chiefly, that a little leaven may leaven the whole lump. (WJW, vol. 13, 36)

Stated Intention (Matt. 13:34–35)

Matthew now inserts a word of insight to the reader. These verses tell us **Jesus spoke all these things to the crowd in parables; he did not say anything to them without using a parable** (v. 34). This was His method, and no one ever used the method more effectively than our Lord. But effectiveness was not the only reason Jesus used parables. He spoke in parables in fulfillment of a prophetic psalm: **I will open my mouth in parables, I will utter things hidden since the creation of the world** (v. 35; see Ps. 78:2). Thus, we have another indication of His indeed being the Messiah, the long-awaited One sent to bring hope and salvation to these who heard His words.

Sound Investment (Matt. 13:44)

This parable is actually quite simple, likening **the kingdom of heaven** to a **treasure hidden in a field.** A man finds it, hides it, and then is so full of joy that he divests himself of all his possessions that he might buy the field where he found the treasure.

We know by Jesus' explanation of the parable of the weeds in verses 36–43 some facts about this parable. First, the man is the "Son of Man" (v. 37). Second, "the field is the world" (v. 38). By grammatical structure, we know that the treasure is the **kingdom of heaven** (v. 44). God put all He had on the line to provide salvation for the whole world, to the end that He might redeem the church, now the Israel of God, this great treasure worth more than all the material world. All of this He did through Jesus Christ.

The treasure may still be hidden from time to time, but we have already seen that, even in its quietness, its influence is still realized. One of these days, the church will be revealed in all its glory and splendor, and it will be proven once and for all that God's investment was a sound one.

WORDS FROM WESLEY
Matthew 13:44

The kingdom of heaven is like treasure hid in a field—The kingdom of God within us, is a treasure indeed, but a treasure hid from the world, and from the most wise and prudent in it. He that *finds* this treasure (perhaps when he thought it far from him) hides it deep in his heart, and gives up all other happiness for it. (ENNT)

Sparkling Insight (Matt. 13:45–46)

In this parable, we shift our imaginations into another gear. Until now in these passages, the kingdom of heaven has been likened to inanimate objects. Here we are told that **the kingdom**

of heaven is like a merchant (v. 45)—a person, not a thing. This is not just any man; he is a **merchant looking for fine pearls.** In Jesus' day, the people recognized the pearl as one of the most desirable of all possessions. Down by the Red Sea was the best place to find the finest pearls of that area of the world. Jesus grabbed the people's attention quickly when He spoke of finding fine pearls. **When he found one of great value, he went away and sold everything he had and bought it** (v. 46). This one stood out above all the rest. The merchant could not be distracted by lesser pearls once he had found the one of greater beauty and value.

The teaching here focuses on the church's response to such lavish grace demonstrated in the parable just before it. God gave all He had in Christ to provide salvation for the whole world, that He might raise out of it this wonderful treasure called the church. Now the church must give heed to its response to such extravagant expression of love. Again, going back to our grammar lessons, the merchant is the church (the kingdom of heaven). The church must not get distracted by lesser things than the highest purpose God has for it. There are many fine and beautiful things with which the church may involve itself. The pursuit of knowledge is a noble cause, one that has brought much satisfaction to many; but knowledge, with all its loveliness, is a lesser pearl. The church has many times been caught up in correction of social ills, and its voice ought to be heard concerning many of these causes; however, championing social causes is not the greatest pearl it can find, no matter how lovely it may seem. The most valuable, the loveliest of all the pearls to be found is to discover, accept, and accomplish the will of God for our lives. This is not to diminish the value of all the other pearls we may see along the way; but none can surpass the value of this great pearl. When all is said and done, we will be held accountable for how we carried out the will of God in our lives, not how much we could learn or how many causes we could champion. Nothing is more valuable to the Christian's focus in life than knowing, accepting, and doing the will of God gladly. That is true wisdom and insight for holy living.

Sure Ingathering (Matt. 13:47–50)

The kingdom of heaven is like a net that was let down into the lake and caught all kinds of fish (v. 47). This net (called a dragnet) was not kept on the shore for show, but was put to its intended use—catching fish. The parable goes to tell us that it eventually **was full**; at that point **the fishermen pulled it up on the shore . . . sat down and collected the good fish in baskets, but threw the bad away** (v. 48). Again this was a picture Jesus' listeners would recognize as a common happening. The net, with its lead weights placed around the edge, was let down behind the boat. As the boat was propelled through the water, the net would fill up with all kinds of fish, other creatures, seaweed, and debris. When it was full, the fishermen had to sort the catch, keeping the good fish and throwing away everything else.

This is the only parable in this particular collection for which we have a clear interpretation. Jesus said the picture seen here is **how it will be a the end of the age** (v. 49). Judgment is coming. On that day, **the angels will come and separate the wicked from the righteous and throw them into the fiery furnace** (vv. 49–50). Good grain and weeds may grow together for a while, all kinds of debris and creatures and good fish may be in the net until the net almost breaks, but there comes a time for sorting, separating the good from the bad. It will certainly pay to be among the righteous, God's holy people at that day; if not, the end will be terrible.

In Matthew 13, we are given several parables, each one showing a different aspect of the kingdom of heaven. As we look at the collection we have considered here, we can say this: Even though it may be small in its beginnings, sometimes silent for awhile, the kingdom of heaven, God's church, is so precious that God gave all He could to redeem it, and one day it will be gathered to spend eternity with Him; therefore, no price is too great to be certain that we remain focused on knowing, accepting, and accomplishing His perfect will in the world—the perpetuation of this wonderfully blessed church—His own people.

WORDS FROM WESLEY

Matthew 13:47

A great net the gospel is,
Which cast into the sea
Sinners draws out of the' abyss
Of sin and misery.
Good and bad promiscuous hear,
The sacraments alike partake,
Till that final day appear,
And Christ the difference make.
Holy and unholy now
The outward church compose,
But our Lord the heavens shall bow,
And part His friends and foes:
Clothed with boundless power Divine,
We know Thou wilt to judgment come,
Severally to each assign
His just, eternal doom. (PW, vol. 10, 187)

DISCUSSION

We often seek visible results, but one life redeemed can impact many generations.

1. Jesus' usual practice in teaching was storytelling, according to Matthew 13:34. Why do you think He chose this method of communicating?

2. Summarize the central point in each of these parables.

3. Can you think of other verses that show how the smallest and least become great in the kingdom of God?

4. Contrast the treasure in the field with a modern-day treasure that might be difficult to give up.

5. Compare Jesus telling stories with alternative methods of sharing the gospel, like technology.

6. How would you explain that the gospel of Christ is more valuable than another work, such as Confucius' morals or Plato's philosophy?

7. Does God still offer supernatural wisdom and guidance to us today? If so, how?

8. Why do some despise small beginnings?

9. Name something that competes with Christ for your love or service.

10. What is your vision for growth for yourself, for your family, and for your church?

PRAYER

Heavenly Father, open our eyes to see Your work in and around us. Amen.

11

GIVING AND RECEIVING FORGIVENESS

Matthew 18:21–35

It is possible for you to forgive.

True or false: Some people have been hurt so deeply that it is impossible for them to forgive those who have harmed them.

While most of us would say that statement is false on an intellectual level, in practical terms we may find ourselves agreeing. Is it possible to forgive an adulterer? A murderer? A child molester? Many of us would admit that we're just not sure.

Yet our willingness to forgive others is critical to our ability to receive forgiveness from God. We may have been wronged by others, but we have also been in the wrong. We have been forgiven, and we must forgive.

This study will apply that essential truth to your life and help you take the next step in giving or receiving forgiveness.

COMMENTARY

Each of the gospel writers focused on a different aspect of the character and ministry of Jesus. Matthew was particularly interested in helping his readers see Jesus as Israel's Messiah King. Thus, he included in his gospel many references as to how Jesus was the fulfillment of Old Testament Scriptures as well as a number of Jesus' parables about the kingdom of heaven.

Jesus' ministry began with the announcement by both John and Jesus that "The kingdom of heaven is near" (Matt. 3:2; 4:17). Matthew used the phrase "kingdom of heaven" thirty-three times and "kingdom of God" four times, while the other gospel writers used "kingdom of God" in every case. Nevertheless, the two phrases are essentially synonymous. Because of the way they are used, they refer more to the ruling activity of God than to the realm over which He rules. In that sense, the kingdom of heaven then was both an eschatological event that would be fully realized at the end of the age as well as a present reality ushered in by the activity and teachings of Jesus.

Matthew 18 begins with a question posed by the disciples: "Who is the greatest in the kingdom of heaven?" Jesus answered this question by pointing to children around Him, telling about the need to emulate their humility as well as the necessity of setting a godly example. He told the disciples about how highly God valued them, like a shepherd who would leave ninety-nine sheep on the hills to look for the one that wandered off. He also told them about the necessity of working for reconciliation with people who had offended them.

When Peter heard Jesus talk about the sins of an offending brother, it triggered in his mind a question about forgiveness. He wanted to know how many times one was required to forgive someone. Jesus' answer to this question came, as usual, in the form of a parable, this one about an unmerciful servant. Matthew is the only gospel to record this particular parable, although Luke makes reference to two debtors who were each forgiven a debt in Luke 7:41–43. In this parable, Jesus pointed once again to the kingdom of heaven.

The Question (Matt. 18:21–22)

Peter's question to Jesus was very simple. He asked, **"Lord, how many times shall I forgive my brother when he sins against me? Up to seven times?"** (v. 21). It was a typical question of a disciple to a rabbi. And it is a common question of people today, as well. Perhaps Peter had in mind the common response of forgiving a person three times for an offense, but on the fourth time to withhold forgiveness (see Amos 2:6). But as a disciple of Jesus, Peter thought that perhaps his forgiveness should be more generous, even up to seven times. Possibly, but unlikely, the number seven denoted for him the sense of complete forgiveness.

Jesus' response, though, was unexpected and hyperbolic. **"I tell you, not seven times, but seventy-seven times"** (Matt. 18:22). Another possible rendering of this text is "seventy times seven." Whichever number Jesus referred to, it was a huge contrast to Peter's generous offer of seven times. By giving Peter that number, Jesus did not mean for him to keep counting until it was finally achieved. After all, true forgiveness is not really a matter of celestial arithmetic. It is limitless. God forgave us far beyond our comprehension. And because of that, there should be no limit to a believer's forgiveness of others.

Perhaps one reason Jesus gave Peter such a huge number to measure his forgiveness was because of his, and our, difficulty with forgetting. When God forgives, He forgets the offense completely. "I, even I, am he who blots out your transgressions, for my own sake, and remembers your sins no more" (Isa. 43:25). It is not as easy for us to forget. The memory of past hurts keeps coming back to haunt us—sometimes long after we have forgiven someone. And each time it does, it reminds us afresh that we have a responsibility to keep on forgiving. Once will not be enough. Neither will two or three times. Not even seven times. But eventually, somewhere on the way to seventy-seven, the offense will eventually be forgotten.

Jesus was a master storyteller, so He did not let His hyperbolic statement to forgive seventy-seven times simply stand alone. Instead, He used this occasion to give His disciples another picture for the kingdom of heaven. Jesus frequently used His parables to give His disciples a picture of himself. Here, for the first time, He portrayed himself as a king, while His disciples were portrayed as bondservants with whom He will ultimately settle accounts.

The Example of a King (Matt. 18:23–27)

The central figure in Jesus' story was **a king who wanted to settle accounts with his servants** (v. 23), so he brought one before him **who owed him ten thousand talents** (v. 24). This was not just a huge sum of money—it was astronomical, by weight over three hundred tons. By present standards, it was equivalent to many millions of dollars. It was similar in value to the amount King David gave from his treasury for the building of the temple (1 Chron. 29:4). It is also the amount Haman offered to give the king of Persia to exterminate the Jews (Est. 3:9). We are not told how the servant came to owe the king such a huge sum of money, but we are told, not surprisingly, that **he was not able to pay** (Matt. 18:25).

With no assets to repay his debt, the king **ordered** (v. 25) that everything he owned be **sold**, even including himself and his wife and children. This was a common means of exacting payment in the ancient world, as seen in the example of a widow in Elisha's day (2 Kings 4:1). But considering the sum the man owed, this would be no more than a drop in the bucket against the debt. The king's action against his servant shows that he was very angry with him.

WORDS FROM WESLEY

Matthew 18:24

One was brought who owed him ten thousand talents—According to the usual computation, if these were talents of gold, this would amount to seventy-two millions sterling. If they were talents of silver, it must have been four millions, four hundred thousand pounds. Hereby our Lord intimates the vast number and weight of our offences against God, and our utter incapacity of making Him any satisfaction. (ENNT)

We, God's servants, are deeply indebted to Him as well. We have run up a tab on our sin that we will never be able to pay. And ultimately He will demand of us an accounting. When He does, His wrath will be well deserved.

However, this parable does not center on the king's anger but on his mercy. **The servant fell on his knees** (Matt. 18:26), pleading with the king to be patient with him and allow him to pay everything back. He sounds like the proverbial gambling addict pleading with his loan shark for one more chance to "hit the big one." In reality, his chances of succeeding were almost as astronomical as the debt itself. Yet in the middle of this pitiful scene, the king did something highly unexpected—he **canceled the debt and let him go** (v. 27). What king would have forgiven such a huge debt, rightfully owed to him, and let the man go free? Only a divine one, whose quality of mercy perfectly balances His justice!

WORDS FROM WESLEY

Matthew 18:27

Sinners the Lord our God receives,
And never partially forgives,
Whate'er our sins He pardons all,
The great as freely as the small,
When humbly we confess the debt,
And beg forbearance at His feet.
Master, Thou didst the same by me,
When at Thy feet I lay;
Thy grace forgave, and set me free,
And left me nought to pay:
The full discharge of all my debt
I thankfully receive,
And thus my fellow-servants treat,
And thus like Thee forgive. (PW, vol. 10, 319–320)

The Response of the Servant (Matt. 18:28–31)

One would think that, after being forgiven such a huge debt, this servant would have wanted to act mercifully toward others. But Jesus said that when he went away from the king, the servant immediately went and found a fellow servant who owed him **a hundred denarii** (v. 28), the equivalent of a few dollars. Jesus said that **he grabbed him and began to choke him**, demanding to be paid back what he was owed.

The fellow servant echoed the request of the first servant when he had been before the king—**Be patient with me and I will pay you back** (v. 29). The tiny amount he was owed by his fellow servant was minuscule by comparison to that which he himself had owed the king. And, unlike him, his fellow servant could have eventually repaid his debt. This should have triggered a compassionate response, as had been shown him by the king, but instead the servant had his fellow servant **thrown into prison until he could pay the debt** (v. 30). He was in his rights to do so, legally. But morally, an example and a standard had been set for him. Consequently, when **other servants saw what had happened, they were greatly distressed** and reported it back to the king (v. 31).

The King's Justice (Matt. 18:32–35)

The king was understandably upset when he heard what his servant had done. He called him back in and said, **"You wicked servant . . . I canceled all that debt of yours because you begged me to. Shouldn't you have had mercy on your fellow servant just as I had on you?"** (vv. 32–33). It was a rhetorical question— of course he should have! The king had set the standard. He expected the servant would follow his example.

WORDS FROM WESLEY
Matthew 18:34

His lord delivered him to the tormentors—Imprisonment is a much severer punishment in the Eastern countries than in ours. State criminals, especially when condemned to it, are not only confined to a very mean and scanty allowance, but are frequently loaded with clogs or heavy yokes, so that they can neither lie nor sit at ease: and by frequent scourgings and sometimes rackings are brought to an untimely end. *Till he should pay all that was due to him*—That is, without all hope of release, for this he could never do. (ENNT)

Nevertheless, in response to his servant's lack of forgiveness toward his fellow servant, the king rescinded his own mercy. He had freely offered it to him, but now his servant had in turn set the standard by which he would himself be judged. Instead of mercy for mercy, it would be justice for justice. So, the king **turned him over to the jailers to be tortured, until he should pay back all he owed** (v. 34). And since he was realistically unable to pay it back, he was effectively given a life sentence.

Since this parable was given as an allegory of the kingdom of heaven, Jesus made the application very plain to Peter: **"This is how my heavenly Father will treat each of you unless you forgive your brother from your heart"** (v. 35). As He had declared in the Beatitudes, "Blessed are the merciful, for they will be shown mercy" (Matt. 5:7). And in the prayer He taught His disciples, He prayed and commented, "Forgive us our debts, as we also have forgiven our debtors. . . . For if you forgive men when they sin against you, your heavenly Father will also forgive you. But if you do not forgive men their sins, your Father will not forgive your sins" (Matt. 6:12, 14–15).

We desperately need the mercy of God. In fact, we cannot live without it. But we dare never presume upon that mercy, for there is nothing in us that deserves it. Instead, we deserve His wrath. But in Christ God has extended His mercy to all people, offering to cancel their debt and forgive their sins. Through His death on Calvary, Christ has paid the price for our salvation and set us free. In return, He expects us to serve as agents of His grace in the fallen and broken world in which we live.

WORDS FROM WESLEY

Matthew 18:35

How observable is this whole account; as well as the great inference our Lord draws from it! 1. The debtor was freely and fully forgiven; 2. He wilfully and grievously offended; 3. His pardon was retracted, the whole debt required, and the offender delivered to the tormentors for ever. And shall we still say, but when we are once freely and fully forgiven, our pardon can never be retracted? Verily, verily, I say unto you, *So likewise will my heavenly Father do to* you, *if ye from your hearts, forgive not every one his brother their trespasses.* (ENNT)

Many of God's servants are being tormented today by unforgiveness. They have been hurt in a variety of ways, and rather than extending mercy, they have chosen instead to hang on to their hurts. They think that by withholding forgiveness they are hurting the other person, but in reality they are only hurting themselves. By refusing to forgive, they forfeit God's forgiveness in themselves, and this in turn eats away at their soul. How differently we would live if we really believed that God only forgives us to the extent that we forgive others!

DISCUSSION

Offering and receiving forgiveness is the pathway to true reconciliation.

1. Why do you think Peter may have asked the question about forgiveness?

2. Some translations say "seventy times seven" is how many times we should forgive. Do you think this answer is meant to be taken literally? That is, 490 times? Why or why not?

3. The servant in Jesus' story was in great debt to a king. What circumstances today might be similar to his?

4. What would account for the unforgiving attitude in the servant who failed to forgive?

5. What is the relationship between giving and receiving forgiveness? How does this fit with what you know about the character of God?

6. Share a few reasons why it is hard to forgive.

7. What allowances, if any, does Jesus make for our difficulty in forgiving?

8. How is it that we can sometimes forgive the "big stuff" but allow little things to still bother us?

9. What do you do if you forgive someone but he or she doesn't receive it?

10. Forgiveness allows you to leave one place—bitterness, for example—to go to another. Where do you want forgiveness to take you?

PRAYER

Merciful Father, help us extend forgiveness to others, so we may become more like Your Son. Amen.

12

KEEPING WATCH FOR THE SECOND COMING

Matthew 24:36–51

We must be ready for Christ's return at any time.

Focus, follow through, and finishing well are important in every endeavor from business to sports to child rearing. Yet we lead busy lives filled with distractions and interruptions. It can be challenging to finish well in a game of golf, let alone in the lifelong pursuit of becoming like Christ.

To increase our level of attention, Jesus emphasized the uncertain timing of His return to earth. In fact, He said only the Father knows the exact day and hour. In the interim, we are advised to be effective in the work of representing Him in the world.

This study will increase your level of urgency about the return of Christ and cause you to be more diligent in the stewardship of your time, talent, and treasure.

COMMENTARY

As Jesus left the temple and headed for the Mount of Olives, He told His disciples the stones of the temple would be "thrown down." At the Mount of Olives, the disciples asked, "When will this happen, and what will be the sign of your coming and of the end of the age?" (Matt. 24:3). The discourse that follows is often referred to as the "Olivet Discourse." In verses 4–35, Jesus gave them the signs that will precede His coming: false Christs, wars and rumors of wars, famines and earthquakes, persecution of Christians, a falling away from the faith, deception by false prophets, lack of love, and the gospel preached throughout the world.

In verses 15–28, He warned them in greater detail, continuing in verses 29–35 with signs that accompany the end: disturbances in the sun, moon, and stars; the Son of Man coming on the clouds with power and glory; the trumpet call and the gathering of the elect. When they see these things begin to happen, Jesus said, they would know His coming is near.

But the question that is undoubtedly still in the disciples' minds is "When?" For some reason, all of us are transfixed with the timing of these events. We don't want to know only what is going to happen; we want to know when we can expect them to happen. In verses 36–50, Jesus began to address the question of when. But His answer was not at all what the disciples were expecting.

The Time of Christ's Coming Is Unknown to Us (Matt. 24:36–39, 42)

Notice the emphasis Jesus put on not knowing: **No one knows about that day or hour** (v. 36); **they knew nothing about what would happen** (v. 39); and **you do not know on what day** (v. 42). Many people today claim to know exactly when Christ will return. They have graphs and charts that sometimes even plot the exact day and hour. But Jesus said these things are not for us to know. Does this seem like a contradiction? On the one hand, He told His disciples about all the signs pointing to His coming—"When you see all these things, you know that it is near, right at the door" (v. 33)—yet on the other hand, He didn't want them speculating about exact times.

No one knows the time of Jesus' return, **not even the angels in heaven, nor the Son, but only the Father** (v. 36). It is hard for us to imagine Jesus Christ, part of the Godhead, not knowing something. Surely He was speaking here of His humanity. Jesus let go of all His heavenly glory and omniscience when He "made himself nothing, taking the very nature of a servant, being made in human likeness" (Phil. 2:7). Jesus' lack of knowledge was a self-imposed limit, that He might experience what it is to be truly human. We should not conclude from this statement that He is any less God. The point Jesus made is that if the angels don't know the exact dates and even He does not know, then there is no sense in our striving (and sometimes conniving) to devise a timeline of events. "It is not for you to know the times or dates the Father has set by his own authority" (Acts 1:7).

So, if we cannot know the exact times, why does Jesus bother to tell us about future events at all? First, after having told the disciples about the persecution they would endure, He wanted to assure them (and us) that judgment is certainly coming. Second, He wanted the fact of His future coming to impact how they (and us) live every moment until He comes.

Christ's Coming Judgment Is Certain (Matt. 24:37–41, 50–51)

Although no one knows the day or hour, the Son of Man will come. **As it was in the days of Noah, so it will be at the coming of the Son of Man** (v. 37). The days of Noah were exceedingly wicked. Only eight righteous people were saved on the ark when the floodwaters came. All the rest were taken away in judgment. Jesus said it will be just like that when He comes. People will **be eating and drinking, marrying and giving in marriage** (v. 38)—doing what normal people do every day. Although Noah had warned them of impending disaster, the people of his day carried on their normal business as if nothing were about to happen. In the same way, before Christ returns there will be signs that His coming is near (the signs He listed at the beginning of Matt. 24), but the rest of the world will be oblivious to such signs and will carry on with life just as they always had done. And disaster will overtake them just as it did in the days of Noah: **Two men will be in the field; one will be taken and the other left. Two women will be grinding with a hand mill; one will be**

taken and the other left (vv. 40–41). Jesus, of course, was speaking here of being taken in judgment. The **flood . . . took them all away** (v. 39), meaning the wicked were taken away and only the righteous aboard the ark were left. In the parallel passage in Luke 17:26–37, after Jesus told the disciples that one will be taken, the disciples asked, "Where?" Jesus answered, "Where there is a dead body, there the vultures will gather." He was certainly talking about being taken in judgment.

Some have mistakenly taught that these verses refer to a secret rapture of the church, where the righteous will be taken out of the world so God can send His wrath on the wicked. But these verses do not teach that at all. This is why Jesus used the analogy of the thief in Matthew 24:43. Here and elsewhere Jesus said His coming will be like a thief. Those who interpret these verses as meaning Christ will come to take all Christians to heaven have a hard time explaining why Jesus would use such a negative example. A thief doesn't come to bring joy or reward, but to take away and plunder. Jesus' coming is as a thief to the disobedient and unrepentant. He doesn't come to give life, but to take it in judgment.

WORDS FROM WESLEY

Matthew 24:51

And allot him his portion with the hypocrites—The worst of sinners, as upright and sincere as he was once.

If ministers are the persons here primarily intended, there is a peculiar propriety in the expression. For no hypocrisy can be baser, than to call ourselves ministers of Christ, while we are the slaves of avarice, ambition, or sensuality.—Wherever such are found, may God reform them by His grace, or disarm them of that power and influence, which they continually abuse to His dishonour, and to their own aggravated damnation! (ENNT)

The certainty of coming judgment is also highlighted in verses 50–51: **The master of that servant will come on a day when he does not expect him and at an hour he is not aware of. He will cut him to pieces and assign him a place with the hypocrites, where there will be weeping and gnashing of teeth.** An hour is coming when all those who do evil will reap what they have sown.

Christ's Coming Should Affect How We Live Today (Matt. 24:42–49)

We ignore the teaching of Christ's second coming to our own peril. This passage of Scripture points to the fact that Christ is indeed coming back, and that His coming will be sudden, swift, and unexpected. What should be our response? **Therefore keep watch, because you do not know on what day your Lord will come** (v. 42). We should be living every day as if Christ were coming today. The fact of His coming should impact how we live. Peter described how the world would end and then asked, "Since everything will be destroyed in this way, what kind of people ought you to be? You ought to live holy and godly lives as you look forward to the day of God and speed its coming" (2 Pet. 3:11–12). John said, "We know that when he appears, we shall be like him, for we shall see him as he is. Everyone who has this hope in him purifies himself, just as he is pure" (1 John 3:2–3).

Keeping watch means more than passively standing by and observing. It means to guard vigilantly, just as **the owner of the house . . . would have kept watch and would not have let his house be broken into** (Matt. 24:43). The head of the house would have taken definitive steps to guard his house, just as we must take definitive steps to guard our hearts. **So you also must be ready, because the Son of Man will come at an hour when you do not expect him** (v. 44).

Jesus summed up His teaching by contrasting the possible reactions of a servant. The servant has been given responsibilities in the absence of the Master: He has been **put in charge of the servants in his household to give them their food at the proper time** (v. 45). And he is expected to carry out those responsibilities: **It will be good for that servant whose master finds him doing so when he returns** (v. 46). Jesus expects us to be busy doing His business until He returns. Such a servant is described as **faithful and wise** (v. 45), and because of his actions, the master **will put him in charge of all his possessions** (v. 47). Faithfulness means doing what we're commanded to do until Christ returns. This is the faithfulness God rewards. "For everyone who has will be given more, and he will have an abundance" (Matt. 25:29).

WORDS FROM WESLEY

Matthew 24:45

Who then is the faithful and wise servant—Which of you aspires after this character? *Wise*—Every moment retaining the clearest conviction, that all he now has is only intrusted to him as a steward: to *Faithful*—Thinking, speaking, and acting continually, in a manner suitable to that conviction. (ENNT)

It is highly significant that the three parables that follow Matthew 24:36–51 all address this same issue: being faithful and doing what we ought to do until the coming of the Lord. The parable of the ten virgins (25:1–13) ends with, "Therefore keep watch, because you do not know the day or the hour." The parable of the talents (25:14–30) warns us that God expects us to be faithful by multiplying what He has given to us. The parable of the sheep and the goats (25:31–46) reveals that it is only those who are actively doing something for the Lord—clothing the naked, feeding the hungry, visiting the sick and imprisoned—who are considered faithful and are thereby rewarded. The rest, who refused to do the good they were expected to do, find that only judgment awaits them. Could Jesus make it any clearer that He expects us to be actively doing something until He returns? We must keep watch, be ready, and be faithful and wise.

WORDS FROM WESLEY

Matthew 24:46

Full of earnest expectation,
Look we for our heavenly Lord,
Working out our own salvation,
Labouring for a full reward:
Happy, in the task assign'd us
If we still our lives employ,
Labouring on if Jesus find us,
We shall share our Master's joy. (PW, vol. 10, 379)

We are not to be like the wicked servant who has calculated the timetable and reasons that **my master is staying away a long time** and so chooses to sin (24:48). Little does he realize that the Lord will return unexpectedly and that he will face certain judgment. He reminds us of the fool in Luke 12:16–20 who decides to slack off because of his accumulated wealth. The theme of that passage is greed, but the lesson is the same: Judgment comes unexpectedly. We need to be ready.

Peter warned, "In the last days scoffers will come, scoffing and following their own evil desires. They will say, 'Where is this "coming" he promised? Ever since our fathers died, everything goes on as it has since the beginning of creation.' But they deliberately forget that long ago by God's word the heavens existed and the earth was formed out of water and by water. . . . By the same word the present heavens and earth are reserved for fire, being kept for the day of judgment and destruction of ungodly men" (2 Pet. 3:3–7).

Peter went on to tell us that "with the Lord a day is like a thousand years, and a thousand years are like a day" (3:8). We should not give up hope because Christ has not yet returned. The certainty of His return should prompt us to active obedience and watchfulness.

DISCUSSION

Following Christ means remaining awake and alert while many others are still fast asleep.

1. According to this passage, what things can we know for certain about the return of Jesus?

2. Jesus mentioned events in the time of Noah. In what ways are our times similar to those?

3. Compare what you learned here with what Paul said in 1 Thessalonians 4:16–17.

4. Define *vigilance*.

5. The return of Jesus is mentioned in twenty-three out of twenty-seven New Testament books. Why do you suppose we talk so little about it these days?

6. Describe the lifestyle of a person who is living with the expectation of Christ's return. Describe the lifestyle of someone who is not expecting Christ's return.

7. If you were to hold an open house where everyone could see your heart and actions, how would you prepare?

8. If you felt sure Jesus would return tomorrow, what would you do today?

PRAYER

Lord, help us to "stay awake" and be mindful of Your work in this world. May we live in a state of readiness. Amen.

13

RELATIONAL HOLINESS

Matthew 25:31–46

Our love for Christ will be reflected in our treament of others.

What is the essence of Christianity? Faith, some believers might answer our belief in the resurrection of Jesus Christ. Virtue, others might say; our religion can be described as a godly way of living. Both answers are good, but Jesus' story about sheep and goats gives a clue to what He sees as central to the life of a Christian—our treatment of others, especially those who are in need.

This study explodes the notion that Christianity is a personal matter that can be defined solely by our intellectual beliefs or personal piety and challenges us to do as Jesus did by caring for those in need.

COMMENTARY

The return of Jesus was of great concern to the disciples. In Matthew 24, Jesus revealed conditions leading up to His return and admonished them to be watchful, faithful, and wise. Chapter 25 discloses requirements of those who would be watchful, faithful, and wise. Those who were accepted had kept the greatest commandments: Love God and your neighbor as yourself.

In the parable of the ten virgins, the five foolish ones neglected to be personally prepared. They each chose independently and personally. They lived only for the present and neglected to care for maintenance and the future. They were denied entrance into the feast.

In the parable of the talents, one servant neglected to do anything, though digging a hole and burying the talent would have required more time and energy than taking it to the bank. The master with wisdom had handed out the talents and had entrusted each servant with an amount equal to his ability. The neglectful one's concept of the master was perverted by his own character. The increase in value was not important, but the use of the talent was. Doing nothing brought condemnation.

The foolish virgins *chose* not to be prepared for the future. The men with the talents *chose* to reveal their devotion to the master. In the account of the separation of the sheep and goats, the Judge acts. He separates by discerning where each person belongs. Some people out of all the nations have chosen to live like Christ by doing good deeds.

In order to properly understand this account, we must realize that all the parables depict principles involved in the judgment. One cannot say the judgment is based entirely on doing benevolent and charitable acts. It is not a question of good works, but rather what produced the good works. We must not only choose to be personally prepared with a reservoir of oil and be using the gifts and abilities bestowed upon us by the Lord, but we must choose to cultivate a relationship with Christ that reveals His character and life within us by caring for the needy and fulfilling the commandment to love our neighbor as ourselves.

The Setting (Matt. 25:31–32)

Calvary, with its shame, humiliation, and ultimate crucifixion, is just three days in the future. But Jesus revealed the awesome scene of grandeur and splendor **when the Son of Man comes** (v. 31).

The title **Son of Man** expresses His relationship to humankind and that the judgment will not be biased. He deliberately chose to become flesh and live among humankind. He became well acquainted with the weaknesses and circumstances of each person on the human level. To be judged by One who experienced and understands the human nature adds to the majestic dignity, grandeur, and solemnity of the judgment. He came to be the Savior Redeemer and now returns as almighty God and all-wise Judge, for He **comes in his glory**. The humiliation will be past. He appears as He is *and* was before coming to the earth in the incarnation. Angels announced His birth with singing, and on this day **all the angels** will be with Him as the Judge. What a cloud of witnesses!

WORDS FROM WESLEY

Matthew 25:31

With what majesty and grandeur does our Lord here speak of himself! Giving us one of the noblest instances of the true sublime. Indeed not many descriptions in the sacred writings themselves seem to equal this. Methinks we can hardly read it without imagining ourselves before the awful tribunal it describes. (ENNT)

He has been in heaven on His Father's right hand interceding for us; but when He comes the second time, **he will sit on his throne in heavenly glory** (v. 31). He will sit in supreme authority and power—power that cannot be overruled—as the reigning King. His heavenly glory is all the nature and attributes of God manifested in wisdom, power, authority, perfect holiness, and righteousness. In this context, **all the nations** (v. 32) refers to all peoples of the entire world. They **will be gathered before him**. What a crowd to be judged!

The Separation (Matt. 25:32–33)

And he will separate the people one from another (v. 32). All nations are gathered collectively, but there is an individual separation from among the people. No one is lost in the crowd!

This separation is like **a shepherd** who **separates the sheep from the goats**. Sheep and goats grazed together but were separated at watering times and at night. The shepherd could easily see the difference because of their outward appearance, color, and actions.

In wisdom, the Son of Man discerns the character of each one in the crowd as quickly and accurately as a shepherd would separate his flocks. He makes the separation not on creed, color, or social standing, but on godly character. It is a universal, impartial, and eternally final separation, for He distinguishes and classifies each one perfectly. He puts **the sheep on his right** (v. 33). The right-hand side is the place of favor, honor, acceptance, and blessing. The goats were placed **on the left**, a place of disfavor and rejection.

The Inheritance (Matt. 25:34–40)

Then (v. 34) the one who called himself the Son of Man now declared himself to be **King**. These persons have a relationship to the King and His Father, thus giving them a right to **take** their **inheritance**. An inheritance is a gift or reward that is dependent upon a relationship between the Giver and the recipient. The sheep are heirs of the kingdom. He invites them to **come** and **take** the kingdom.

The **inheritance, the kingdom prepared for you since the creation of the world** (v. 34), reveals the loving and caring character of God the Father. The Father doesn't act impulsively. His purpose from the creation of the world was for humankind to be heirs of His kingdom. The kingdom had been prepared for His people who manifested His characteristics of holiness and love for all.

For I was hungry . . . I was thirsty . . . I was a stranger [foreigner] **and you invited me in** (v. 35). The Eastern custom of hospitality required one to meet the bare necessities of life — food, water, and shelter — for everyone. **I needed clothes . . .**

I was sick . . . I was in prison (v. 36). These were acts of the "second mile." These works reveal the temperament, motives, and virtues of the doer. They are not words or noble thoughts but proof of the condition of the inner person. They imply the supplier has a generous and spontaneous self-sacrificing spirit. The recipient cannot repay his benefactors. They are models of the *agape* love of God. The King identifies himself with the interests and needs of **the least of these brothers of mine** (v. 40), all the suffering humanity of the world. Jesus walked in the sandals of the homeless who needed food, water, and shelter. Jesus resides in the destitute, afflicted, and isolated persons.

Lord, when did we see you . . . ? (vv. 37–39). The King vicariously identifies himself in the needy, deprived, and repulsive. The righteous had been living so closely to Him that His character and actions of love were a part of them. They did what the love of Christ compelled them to do. They had done nothing out of the ordinary. They were simply demonstrating godly character. God loves; God sees value in every person, and therefore God responds to the need.

WORDS FROM WESLEY

Matthew 25:35

All these works of outward mercy suppose faith and love, and must needs be accompanied with works of spiritual mercy. But works of this kind the Judge could not mention in the same manner. He could not say, I was in error, and ye recalled me to the truth; I was in sin, and ye brought me to repentance. *In prison*—Prisoners need to be visited above all others, as they are commonly solitary and forsaken by the rest of the world. (ENNT)

Perhaps it was not so much surprise on their part as humility that something as insignificant as a cup of water would be considered great enough for a commendation from the King.

It is not the acts of kindness and expressed sympathy for needy humanity that are rewarded: **whatever you did . . . you did for me** (v. 40). These righteous ones loved Christ. If He were walking among them and needed a lunch, a cup of water, or a room for the night, or if He were ill and needed a visit, or encouragement while in jail, it would have been a joy for them to do these things for Him. But He is not physically present. However, these same acts can be done for Him by meeting the needs of the **least of these brothers** (v. 40), His suffering humanity. This kind of service meets the requirements of the inheritance.

The Sentencing (Matt. 25:41–46)

Then he will say to those on his left (v. 41). They had witnessed and listened to the commendations of those on the right. Now the King turns to them. Note the contrasts between the two groups in verses 34 and 41.

Depart from me (v. 41). They are commanded to leave the presence of the King. They are **cursed** because they chose not to have a relationship that entitled them to an inheritance. The lack of this relationship caused them to be unable to see or be aware of opportunities to serve Jesus by doing good to the unfortunate. They were to depart to a place **prepared for the devil and his angels**. This place was not for humans. John Wesley said "humans are invaders" in this place.

You gave me nothing (v. 42). They had given absolutely nothing, in contrast with "you gave me something" of the righteous ones. Those who are callously indifferent to human needs are unaware that Jesus has a vital relationship with all humanity. **They also will answer** (v. 44). They knew Jesus. They called Him "Lord." But they were ignorant that living for and with Him resulted in aiding those in need. They were not available when the needy were present. **When did we see . . . ?** They ask the same question as those on the right. The King gives the same answer.

Their sin was **whatever you did not do** (v. 45). Doing nothing condemns. They were judged on the evil of not having a relationship with God and also for not establishing a good relationship with others. They never saw the needy because they were not in a right relationship with God. Perhaps they sought self-justification for their lack of sympathy for the needy. But the Judge reveals that to neglect the afflictions of the needy, to disregard the repulsively ill, and to ignore the despised prisoner is to disregard the King.

Eternal punishment and **eternal life** (v. 46) are woefully unlike, and yet the term *eternal* applies to both punishment and life. Eternal life begins in the believer when a relationship with Christ is established, but is unending if the relationship is unbroken. Punishment may not begin until this judgment day, but it is also unending. The acts of mercy and grace done or not done in this present life indicate the choice one has made. This choice determines our eternal destiny either to be able to take our rightful inheritance of eternal life in the kingdom prepared for us or to depart and be an intruder into the place of eternal punishment prepared for the Devil. The decisions made before this judgment day are final, irreversible, and unending.

WORDS FROM WESLEY

Matthew 25:46

And these shall go away into everlasting punishment, but the righteous into life everlasting—Either therefore the punishment is strictly eternal, or the reward is not. The very same expression being applied, to the former as to the latter. The Judge will speak first to the righteous, in the audience of the wicked. The wicked shall then go away into everlasting fire, in the view of the righteous. Thus the damned shall see nothing of the everlasting life. But the just will see the punishment of the ungodly. It is not only particularly observable here, 1, That the punishment lasts as long as the reward: But 2, That this punishment is so far from ceasing at the end of the world, that it does not begin till then. (ENNT)

DISCUSSION

Our love for God empowers and is reflected in our love for others.

1. The sheep are placed to the right. In what other ways does Scripture deem the right as a place of honor?

2. In John 19:13, Pilate sat in a judgment seat. Contrast that with the judgment seat of Christ.

3. Psalm 14:6 states that the Lord is a shelter for the poor. What does that mean?

4. Why would Jesus judge people for what they *didn't* do?

5. If your primary spiritual gift is *not* mercy or giving, how does this passage apply to you?

6. Share several ways we can demonstrate our love for Christ by meeting the tangible needs of others.

7. Do you agree or disagree that you shouldn't give money to a homeless person because he or she will only use it for drugs or alcohol? Why or why not?

8. What is the connection between love of God and love of others? In what other Bible passages do you see this connection made?

9. Explain one way in which you might overlook or ignore a needy person in plain sight.

10. Tell about a time you were in need but didn't share it for fear of rejection.

PRAYER

Father, help us to live like Your sheep. Amen.

WORDS FROM WESLEY WORKS CITED

ENNT: *Explanatory Notes upon the New Testament,* by John Wesley, M.A. Fourth American Edition. New York: J. Soule and T. Mason, for the Methodist Episcopal Church in the United States, 1818.

JJW: *The Journal of the Rev. John Wesley, A.M.* Standard. Edited by Nehemiah Curnock. 8 vols. London: Robert Culley, Charles H. Kelley, 1909–1916.

LCW: *The Life of the Rev. Charles Wesley, M.A., by Thomas Jackson.* 2 vols. London: John Mason, at the Wesleyan Conference Office, 1841.

PW: *The Poetical Works of John and Charles Wesley.* Edited by D. D. G. Osborn. 13 vols. London: Wesleyan-Methodist Conference Office, 1868.

WJW: *The Works of John Wesley.* Third Edition, Complete and Unabridged. 14 vols. London: Wesleyan Methodist Book Room, 1872.

OTHER BOOKS IN THE
WESLEY BIBLE STUDIES SERIES

Genesis (available February 2015)
Exodus (available April 2015)
Leviticus through Deuteronomy (available June 2015)
Joshua through Ruth (available June 2015)
1 Samuel through 2 Chronicles (available February 2015)
Ezra through Esther (available April 2015)
Job through Song of Songs (available February 2015)
Isaiah (available April 2015)
Jeremiah through Daniel (available February 2015)
Hosea through Malachi (available June 2015)
Matthew
Mark
Luke (available September 2014)
John (available April 2014)
Acts (available September 2014)
Romans (available June 2014)
1–2 Corinthians (available September 2014)
Galatians through Colossians and Philemon (available June 2014)
1–2 Thessalonians (available September 2014)
1 Timothy through Titus (available April 2014)
Hebrews (available April 2014)
James
1–2 Peter and Jude (available April 2014)
1–3 John (available June 2014)
Revelation (available June 2014)

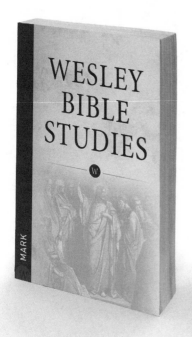
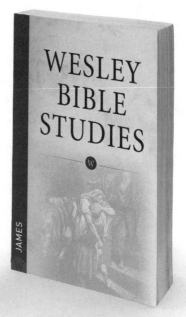